COLLINS POCKET REFERENCE

WEDDINGS

The Diagram Group

HarperCollins*Publishers*

HarperCollins Publishers
P.O. Box, Glasgow G4 0NB

A Diagram book first created by Diagram Visual Information
Limited of 195 Kentish Town Road, London NW5 8SY

First published 1994

Reprint 10 9 8 7 6 5 4

© Diagram Visual Information Limited 1994

ISBN 0 00 470540 8

A catalogue record for this book is available
from the British Library

Printed in Hong Kong

Introduction

For many people, the prospect of organizing a wedding
is a daunting one that requires careful planning. With
the numerous challenges in mind, *Collins Pocket
Reference Weddings* is designed to help the prospective
bride and groom with the choices they need to make
and the responsibilities they may have to assume.

Engagement and the legal aspects of getting married are
dealt with first of all. Types of religious ceremony that
take place, and the procedures that a bridal couple are
required to follow when arranging church and register
office weddings, are then detailed. Advice is also
offered on arranging the reception and the invitations,
organizing the flowers and photography, and preparing
for the honeymoon. Further chapters illustrate the
responsibilities of the bride and groom, and the duties
assumed by the bride's parents and attendants.

One innovative feature of this book is the information
given on the traditions and customs underlying many
aspects of the wedding preparations and ceremony.
Engagements of old and the 'plighting of troth', the
links between fertility and the wedding cake, and the
associations between certain colours and the bride's
dress are just a few of the topics investigated.

With helpful checklists, summaries and countdown
charts included throughout, *Collins Pocket Reference
Weddings* is an invaluable guide for all those involved
in planning and organizing a wedding.

Acknowledgements

The following are gratefully acknowledged for the help
and information provided regarding marriage and the
law, and register office weddings:

Marriages and General section
of the General Register Office

Simon Hudson,
Superintendent Registrar,
Harrow

Stuart Assur,
Registrar,
Glasgow

Contents

1. Engagement

ENGAGEMENTS OF OLD

The engagement is a means to an end: marriage.
Indeed, the full term is 'engaged to be married'; the
state has no other purpose. At one time, however, the
engagement was as important as the wedding itself. As
a result, there are many traditions and customs
associated solely with the engagement period, some of
which survive today.

When women were 'chattel'

Not so long ago, women were regarded as first their
father's, then their husband's 'chattel' or property.
Many of the traditions that are maintained today have
their roots in this view of women, even if this view is
now out of date.

Anglo-Saxon men were used to stealing away their
brides-to-be; romance, wooing, and engagements were
not in the picture. But the families of the women
insisted on being reimbursed for what was, after all, a
working member of the family, and thus the tradition of
the 'bride price' was established. The engagement itself
signified the intended transfer of 'ownership' from
father to husband and also provided a period during
which the 'bride price' could be agreed. Several
centuries later, the situation was reversed and fathers
were paying future sons-in-law – or their families – a
'dowry' to marry off their daughters. The engagement
was again a time for agreeing the payment, or dowry,
but also for collecting an extravagant trousseau, at least
for wealthy brides. Today, the engagement period is

more likely to be used for planning the wedding ceremony and arranging for married life.

Finding a mate

Arranged marriages were, and still are, the practice in some cultures; in fact, associating marriage with love is a fairly recent, and for the most part Western, phenomenon. Among Hindus in India, the bride was sometimes selected by drawing lots; one custom involved asking a potential bride to choose one from among four balls of earth taken from four different places. If she selected the ball made of earth from a cemetery, she was rejected by the groom.

In many societies and cultures in which marriages were arranged, there was usually one person – acceptable to both families – who acted as matchmaker. In Korea, this person is often a professional go-between who performs this service for many families. Social and economic status were the primary factors in making a match; it was assumed that love, if it ever happened, would grow with time between the married partners. In other societies, of course, love is expected to come before marriage and to grow stronger over a period of courtship before marriage is proposed. In these days, couples are more likely to choose their own marriage partners, rather than have them selected by family or matchmakers.

Gaining permission

In the past, a man would first approach the family of the woman he intended to marry, and only proceed with the proposal of marriage once he had received the family's permission. Although the practice is no longer customary, some grooms-to-be still carry out a less

formal 'request for the hand' by having a friendly talk
with their future in-laws.

Once the proposal was made and accepted, the
engagement was often marked with a formal ceremony,
a tradition that continues today, although usually in a
more casual guise. Under ancient Jewish tradition, the
engagement ceremony occurred when the actual
marriage contract was signed, making it a more solemn
and binding occasion than the wedding itself and a
divorce was required to undo it. Likewise, in isolated
areas of Britain in the fifteenth and sixteenth centuries,
the engagement ceremony was often the only ceremony
that took place among the poor when they married;
actual weddings – and the fees they required – were
much too expensive.

'Plighting troth'

Historically, engagement – or 'betrothal', as it was
more often known – also signified that a man had
'plighted his troth'. He had therefore entered into a
legal obligation which marriage would ratify. Although
women had no say in the business side of the
arrangement, being formally engaged protected them in
law from being jilted and therefore having to return to
the marriage 'market' at a disadvantage.

Until recent legislation on sexual equality, a woman
who had been jilted could sue her former fiancé for
'breach of promise'. Financially, this meant that any
payment or dowry already made over was repaid. It
also had the effect, however, of restoring a woman's
'character' in society, and therefore gave her the
opportunity to make another match.

Today, the woman's 'character' is less of an issue and

men are no longer under any legal obligation when they
'plight their troth'. The decision to marry, therefore, is a
more equal one and one that depends less on financial
than emotional circumstances.

SUPERSTITIONS

At one time it was thought that to be engaged more
than once meant certain damnation.

The groom-to-be often avoided making the proposal
himself but instead sent friends to represent his interests
to his intended bride or her family. On their way to
make this visit, these representatives would observe
certain things which they would interpret as omens for
the future couple. A monk, a blind man, or a pregnant
woman were among the bad omens, signalling that the
representatives should give up their mission. Nanny
goats, a pigeon, or a wolf were among those bringing
good fortune.

One warning for would-be brides was to avoid suitors
whose surnames began with the same letter as their
own, as contained in a well-known rhyme:

> *To change the name, and not the letter,*
> *Is to change for the worse, and not the better.*

CUSTOMS

One custom from medieval Brittany required the suitor
to leave a branch of hawthorn at the door of his
intended bride on the first day of May. If the woman
accepted his proposal, she would leave the branch; if
she refused, she would replace the branch with the head
of a cauliflower.

Other signs of a rejected proposal were an upside-down frying pan in the fireplace, or flat cakes being served by the woman's mother.

On bended knee
The traditional way in which to make a marriage proposal was for the groom to make his appeal on bended knee, and for the bride to accept gracefully. Modern marriage proposals, however, are usually made in a less romantic fashion.

Accepted proposals were often validated by the engaged couple closing their fists, entwining their little fingers, drinking from one glass or cutting bread with one knife. To break off the engagement later, the woman would give the knife to her rejected suitor.

CHOOSING A DATE

Once engaged, the next big decision for most couples is when to marry. Spring and summer have long been popular seasons. A June wedding, for example, was considered to guarantee a happy marriage. A wedding in May, on the other hand, was thought to bring bad luck. Even the days of the week hold associations for the superstitious: early in the week – Monday, Tuesday and Wednesday – is meant to be better for good fortune than later. Friday, especially Friday the 13th, is considered a very unlucky day to be married. One variation of a famous old rhyme assigns a different omen to every day:

> *Monday for wealth,*
> *Tuesday for health,*
> *Wednesday, the best day of all;*
> *Thursday for crosses,*
> *Friday for losses,*
> *Saturday, no luck at all.*

Saturday has long been the most popular day to be married, presumably because that is a day on which most guests can attend.

In Hindu tradition, an astrologer is consulted to draw up and examine the horoscopes of the bride and groom to determine the most auspicious date, and even the time, of the wedding.

REASONS FOR AN ENGAGEMENT

The engagement period has two main functions: to announce that the couple has made a commitment and is no longer in the 'marriage market', and to prepare for the coming wedding. But it is not a necessity, only a convention, although most couples feel their marriage intentions are more 'real' if they are cemented by an engagement.

Reasons *not* to get engaged

One reason *not* to get engaged is if either or both parties do not want to feel 'left out' because friends have taken this step. Nor is it wise to announce an engagement without any clear idea of whether a subsequent marriage will take place or not. Being engaged is not just the giving and receiving of a ring, it is a serious statement of commitment.

Neither is it a good reason to get engaged because relatives and friends 'expect it'. Perhaps a couple have been seeing each other for a year or two when, gradually, hints are dropped about engagement. It is not for others to decide when a couple is ready to make the commitment to marry. Each couple, even the individual man and woman, is different, and will respond to feelings of love or deep attachment over vastly differing periods. Some will 'know' after only a few weeks, others will need years. What is most important is that the couple concerned feel confident that they have made the right decision without being pressured from outside.

ANNOUNCING THE ENGAGEMENT
Who to tell first
Nevertheless, a couple should always be sensitive to the feelings of, particularly, their parents. The person their child chooses to marry will have been a constant source of worry to them. Will he or she treat their child well? Are they really suited? Questions like these always preoccupy parents, and so a wise couple will not confirm their parents' worst fears by allowing the engagement to come as a shock.

Preventing hurt parental feelings
In most relationships, the parents have already met, and may have become fond of, their child's regular boyfriend or girlfriend. The engaged couple will avoid any hurt feelings, however, if they make sure their parents are the first to know of their decision. After all, in the coming months before the marriage, it may well be the parents who foot the bill for the celebrations, or at least provide help and support before the wedding, and maybe beyond.

Obtaining the bride's father's permission
Traditionally, the man approaches his intended bride's father for permission to marry his daughter, whereupon the prospective father-in-law assesses, by means of close questioning, whether the man is a suitable lifelong partner. This convention may still be observed, but in a more relaxed way, perhaps as an informal chat between the two men.

If parental opposition is expected
Telling their parents first should also hold for those couples who are expecting opposition. Keeping an engagement a secret may well reinforce parental

suspicions that the couple are unsuited; but, more
importantly, the couple should not be afraid of
declaring their intentions – if their feelings are strong
enough. Very often, hostile parents come to respect
their children's decision if it is shown to have been
made responsibly.

Arranging for both sets of parents to meet
If circumstances allow, it would be an appreciated
gesture for the engaged couple to arrange for both sets
of parents to meet and get to know each other. In many
cultures, this goes without saying. If nothing else, such
a meeting breaks the ice and would mean that, on the
wedding day, the parents are not confronted with total
strangers.

MAKING THE ANNOUNCEMENT
Private announcement
Once the close family are party to their decision, a
couple is usually keen to tell as many people as they
think are concerned. If their social circle is small, they
will probably do this by word of mouth. But if their
families are extended and their friends live in distant
parts of the country, then an individual letter (rather
than a telephone call) brings a touch of courtesy to the
message.

Public announcement
Some people, however, wish the whole world – or as
much of it as they can reach – to know of their
intentions, and post an announcement in the local, or
even the national, press. In this case, a telephone call or
letter to the appropriate department – usually the
'Births, marriages and deaths' column – with the

desired message and date of appearance is all that needs to be done. It is worth checking the rates beforehand. A lengthy message which does not really convey any more than a brief announcement could end by being costly.

Who makes the public announcement?

Conventionally, it is the bride's parents who announce the engagement of their daughter – the couple do not announce it themselves unless they are older or embarking on a second marriage. Therefore, a public notice should be worded as shown below.

Whatever the means chosen, the couple should bear in mind that family and friends are eager to share their happiness, and so the most important aspect is making sure everyone is informed individually.

St Peter's church, St Ives
MR AND MRS ROBERTS of Heavitree, Devon, are delighted to announce the engagement of their daughter Margaret to Trevor, son of Kathleen and David Black of Dagenham, Essex.

THE ENGAGEMENT RING

The most visible sign of an engagement is the ring which, traditionally, the prospective groom offers to his fiancée as a token of her promise to marry him. It is worn on the third finger of the left hand, where the wedding ring will be placed at the time of the marriage.

Mounting and setting stones

Gemstones can be set and mounted in a number of styles. Although each style has the practical function of holding the stones in place, some of the settings have also become design elements in their own right. Fashion and other factors, such as the development of more complex manufacturing techniques, have also affected style.

Some variations in the style of setting and mounting gemstones are shown (right).

1 Bezel setting
2 Claw setting
3 Riveting
4 Graining
5 Flush setting
6 Invisible setting (used for pearls)

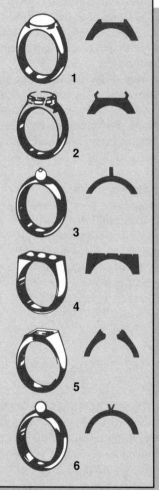

Conventionally, engagement rings are dress rings – that is, they have a gemstone. The difference is in value. The engagement ring is usually the best quality gold, silver or platinum affordable set with precious stones, and it is one of the pleasures of the occasion for the couple to go out and choose the ring of their dreams.

Choosing the ring

Even today, the most popular choice for an engagement ring is the solitaire diamond. The reason for its popularity in former times was its scarcity and durability ('diamonds are forever' is no mere advertising slogan) which matched the rarity and constancy of the love declared between a man and a woman.

The band

The band does not have to be gold. Many couples opt for platinum, a whitish metal even more precious than gold, and some choose white or red gold for variety. Gold comes in different weights and values, measured in carats. Pure gold has 24 carats, but is usually too soft to stand up to normal wear and tear, although most Indian jewellery is 24-carat. The purest gold recommended for rings is 22-carat, then 18-carat and, finally, 9-carat. The lower the carat value, the less gold in the ring. It does not matter which is chosen, the sentiments remain the same. However, when choosing the carat value of the engagement ring, the couple should look ahead to the wedding ring they might choose. This should have the same carat value as the engagement ring. Otherwise, as the rings are usually worn together, the softer metal risks being eroded by the harder one over the years.

The stone

Many couples today are adventurous, and seek out stones
which have novelty value, although they may not be as
precious as the traditional gem stones, such as diamond,
ruby, emerald and sapphire. Stones such as topaz, opal,
garnet and turquoise are also birthstones, and may be
chosen for this special significance. The 'stone', however,
does not have to be a stone as such; for example, pearls
are often chosen, especially a solitaire.

Birthstones

For those who would like to choose a birthstone for
their engagement ring, perhaps to give it extra
significance, the list (below) shows which gems are
associated with which months of the year.

Birthstones and their meaning

Month	Stone	Meaning
January	Garnet	Constancy
February	Amethyst	Sincerity
March	Bloodstone	Courage
April	Diamond	Lasting love
May	Emerald	Hope, success
June	Pearl	Health
July	Ruby	Love
August	Sardonyx	Married happiness
September	Sapphire	Wisdom
October	Opal	Hope
November	Topaz	Faithfulness
December	Turquoise	Harmony

Cutting stones

Precious stones (diamonds, emeralds, sapphires and rubies) are cut into multi-faceted shapes that increase their internal 'fire' or sparkle. This is also done with some hard, semi-precious stones such as amethyst, beryl, zircon and tourmaline. Softer stones, or stones with no internal 'fire', such as coral, opal, lapis lazuli, tiger's eye, agate and bloodstone are cut into a smooth shape known as a cabochon. Different cuts suit different stones as they capitalise on the stone's internal structure.

The most common stone cuts are shown (right) from the top, and from the side.

1 Cabochon cut.
2 Baguette cut, particularly suitable for emeralds and sapphires.
3 Rose cut, a cut which leaves numerous triangular surfaces.
4 Trap cut, a simple squared-off cut.
5 Antique cushion, a fancy cut for rectangular stones.
6 Brilliant cut, which is most commonly used for diamonds.
7 Fancy cut, used to facet pear-shaped stones.

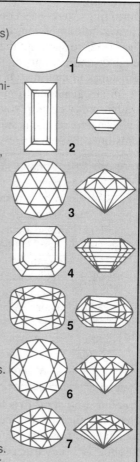

Motto rings

Motto rings were very common in Victorian times,
when overt expressions of sentiment were encouraged!
The idea is to spell out the name of the loved one, or a
suitable sentiment, using the initial letters of the
gemstones in the ring. Of course this idea is limited by
the initials available from desirable gemstones, but it is
a rather pretty custom you might like to try and imitate
if your name, or his, is suitable – or you could use
gemstones that represent your two sets of initials.

DEAREST	diamond, emerald, amethyst, ruby, emerald, sapphire, topaz
REGARD	ruby, emerald, garnet, amethyst, ruby, diamond
PETER	pearl, emerald, topaz, emerald, ruby
GEORGE	garnet, emerald, opal, ruby, garnet, emerald
ROBERT	ruby, opal, beryl, emerald, ruby, tourmaline
SARA	sapphire, amethyst, ruby, amethyst
DEBRA	diamond, emerald, beryl, ruby, amethyst
CAROL	coral, amethyst, ruby, opal, lapis lazuli
ZOE	zircon, opal, emerald
PAM	pearl, amethyst, moonstone

Precious and semi-precious stones

There are numerous stones to choose from for your
engagement ring, and they come in a wide variety of
colours. The only true precious stones are diamonds,
rubies, emeralds and sapphires; all the others are known
as semi-precious or ornamental stones.

Stone	Colour
Agate	banded in different colours
Amethyst	purple
Aquamarine	pale blue-green
Beryl (citrine)	yellow
Bloodstone	green with red flecks
Cameo	white image carved out of pink shell
Cornelian	orange
Chalcedony	white
Chrysoberyl	darkish green
Coral	generally orange, can be red or white
Garnet	purple-red, can be green
Jade	generally green, can be yellow, pink or white
Jasper	brown with coloured flecks
Malachite	banded green
Moonstone	translucent white
Obsidian	black
Onyx	banded black
Opal	white, red or turquoise with rainbow flecks
Pearl	white or pale pink
Rhodonite	pale pink
Rose quartz	pink
Spinel	generally red, can be brown, green or blue
Tiger's eye	banded brown
Topaz	yellow, brown or pink
Tourmaline	generally blue or pink, can be red, brown or green
Zircon	pale blue

A ring for the man?
It is not so usual for the man to have a ring to signify his
engagement, but often the couple like the idea of
exchanging rings and will opt for a signet or similar ring.

CELEBRATING THE ENGAGEMENT
A quiet celebration
Many couples think of the wedding as the occasion to
share with family and friends, and regard their
engagement as intensely personal, to be marked by a
private dinner for two – or even a romantic holiday.
There is nothing antisocial about a couple wanting to be
on their own, and the absence of a big show in no way
diminishes the importance of the occasion.

An engagement party
If the couple belong to a circle which usually celebrates
occasions by throwing a party, however, then their
engagement will be one of the happiest reasons. An
engagement party can be simply a get-together in the
family home (it is usually the woman's parents who
host the party), or a more formal affair at a hall with
caterers.

When to have the celebration
Whatever the couple's decision, the event should not
have to be planned too far in advance, for fear of
coming too close to the wedding. The engagement
party should really be to mark the event and to give
relatives and friends the opportunity to offer their
congratulations – and possibly a gift.

ENGAGEMENT PRESENTS
If the couple holds a party, then almost certainly the
guests will bring a present. It is not usual, however, for

the couple to send round a list as they might for
wedding presents. A list could even seem
presumptuous, and cause offence to the giver. An
engagement present is more of a token of regard than a
major contribution to the future household – perhaps
some special wine glasses, ornaments, small household
items, such as tablemats, or simple jewellery, such as
cufflinks or a bracelet. Whatever is offered should be
acknowledged formally with a thank-you note.

PREPARING FOR MARRIAGE

Once the initial excitement has died down, the serious
business of preparing for marriage gets under way.
This does not exclusively mean organizing the church
or register office, reception and the bride's dress. The
engagement gives a couple the opportunity to talk
honestly about their hopes and fears for the future, and
to try to establish a plan for their life together.

Changes that an engagement brings

These days, it is not uncommon for a couple to have
lived together before the engagement, and therefore to
have experienced day-to-day living with each other and
many of its pitfalls. The engagement changes the
relationship, however. Even though the couple may
have been living together for years, it will have been an
informal arrangement. The engagement heralds the seal
of formality and legality and, as such, is bound to effect
a change in the relationship.

Getting to know each other

Very often, though, the couple will have only been in
each other's company for a few hours a day, at
weekends, or on a fortnight's holiday. They must get

themselves used to the idea that, once married, they
will be together all of their free time, day in, day out.
This is the time to come to terms with previously
unknown features of each other's personality and
habits. These could range from realizing that, much as
he loves you, your partner can't stand early morning
conversations, to something as trivial, yet infuriating, as
never tidying up after himself. Much of a relationship
before the engagement will have been 'courtship'. Both
man and woman will have been on their best behaviour,
and showing themselves in the best possible light,
although probably having the occasional row. The
engagement is a time to realize that nobody is perfect,
and that faults are to be tolerated in everybody.

BREAKING IT OFF
If either one of the couple finds, as the wedding day
gets nearer, that they are having misgivings about some
aspect of their relationship, they should not
automatically dismiss these as owing to 'nerves' or
'pressure'. Almost always this will be the case; but if
doubts persist, even up to the wedding day itself, then
the couple should not be afraid of breaking off the
engagement, even if only temporarily to give
themselves more time. It is far better that they offend
the family than embark upon a long-term relationship
about which they are not one hundred per cent certain.

Telling everybody
If the couple decides this is the best course of action,
then the whole structure of the arrangement has to be
dismantled in the same courteous way in which it was
built up. First, they should tell everybody concerned of

their decision, whether verbally or by letter. There is no need for lengthy explanations. A simple note along the lines of the following will be enough:

> *Susan Atkinson and Bill Dunwoody*
> *regret to inform you that the wedding, arranged for*
> **(day, date, time and place)**
> *will not now take place.*
> *Thank you very much*
> *for your kind thoughts in the past.*

Cancelling the wedding plans

If arrangements have already been made, all the wedding plans should be cancelled. It may seem mercenary to think this way at this distressing time, but there is no point in the couple incurring unnecessary and burdensome expense by making a late cancellation of, say, the reception hall if this can be avoided.

Returning the presents

Next, the couple should offer to return the presents. Most people will not dream of taking them back, but the offer should still be there. After all, they were given as a token of the couple's future life together. Similarly, many people would not want to keep reminders of a happy time that has turned sour.

What to do with the ring

Finally, there is the ring, the obvious symbol of future hopes. There is no hard and fast rule about what to do with it; but, conventionally, if the woman breaks the engagement, she should offer the ring back to her former fiancé. However, if the man ends the engagement, it would be churlish of him to demand his ring back. The woman has every right to keep what is, in effect, a present. But, like the engagement gifts, she may see it as an unhappy reminder and therefore want to give it up.

Post script
Most engagements, however, last the distance, and they provide an exciting period of anticipation that the couple will remember all their lives.

Engagement checklist

- Inform parents first
- Let friends know
- Write to (do not telephone) those who live at some distance
- If required, contact local or national newspapers to put the announcement in their columns
- Carefully select an engagement ring which will hold its value and weather a lifetime's wear.
- Decide on and plan the celebration that is required
  1 none
  2 small family party
  3 large, formal gathering
- Write thank-you notes to those who have given presents
- If the engagement is broken off, remember to cancel all arrangements, offer to return all presents and write to all concerned

Bride and groom's countdown chart

Months in advance

6-12 *Months*

Engagement
- Announce engagement to relatives and friends
- Put announcement in the newspapers
- Choose type of engagement celebration (if wanted)

Marriage ceremony
- Set date, time and discuss wedding plans with the clergyman or rabbi
- Or ensure that the register office is available on the preferred date

Finances
- Meet with both pairs of parents and decide on the budget and responsibilities
- Start getting estimates

Bridesmaids, ushers and best man
- Meet with chief bridesmaid and best man to decide who to select as ushers and bridesmaids
- Decide what you and your attendants will wear

Guest list
- With both sets of parents, make a decision about the number of guests that you would like at the ceremony and at the reception

Reception
- Discuss what you would like, whether you will do the catering or get professionals
- Find out if the preferred venue is available

Floral decorations
- To get ideas and estimates, look around local florists', flower markets, garden centres

Presents
- Start making your wedding list. Read magazines, and visit specialist shops for ideas

Other
- Think about and decide on the theme/style of your wedding
- Think about your honeymoon
- Book time off for the honeymoon

Marriage ceremony
- Decide, with clergyman or rabbi, on a definite date, so that the banns (if you are having a Church of England wedding) may be published. Discuss the type of service (if applicable) you would like to have
- Discuss the order of service and hymns

- If you are having a civil ceremony, make an appointment to see the superintendent registrar exactly 3 months before the wedding date and book the register office

Cars

- Discuss transport arrangements for everyone to church and reception

Reception

- Discuss the type of music you want, and whether you want a band or disco

Floral decorations

- See the florist that you have chosen and discuss what you would like for the church and reception
- Decide about the size and style of the wedding cake you would like

Going away

- Ensure that you have insurance for your honeymoon, that your passports are up to date (if required), and that you have taken out general insurance (see p. 187)

Other

- Find a photographer who will meet your requirements and book him/her
- Begin to shop for wedding rings
- Shop around for and compile the wedding gift list
- Select your wedding rings

Marriage ceremony
- If the order of service still has not been finally decided on, do so now

Going away
- Tidy up any loose ends
- Book a hotel for your wedding night

Clothing
- Finalize arrangements for hire of all outfits, and purchase of wedding dress, arranging final fittings as necessary

Going away
- Ensure that you have suitcases. If not, shop for them

Floral decorations
- Check with the florist that all the arrangements have been made

Other
- Keep other participants informed of progress
- Contact local newspaper for marriage entry and report after the wedding (see 'The bride's mother', p. 241)

Less than a month in advance

Going away

- Buy medicines, sun lotion (if needed), and so on
- Check that you have everything you need

Other

- To make sure that you get the timing right, drive along the route to church (if friends/relatives are driving you) at the same time of day and same day of the week as the ceremony

Marriage ceremony

- Organize a rehearsal at the church

Other

- Ensure that the photographer knows what kind of pictures you want. Find out when you will be able to view the proofs
- Make final checks on all arrangements: reception hall; catering; honeymoon; photographer

Cars

- Put flowers on or in the wedding vehicles

(See also 'Bride's countdown chart', pp. 214-21, and 'Groom's countdown chart', pp.232-5.)

2. Marriage and the law

FORBIDDEN MARRIAGES

In the United Kingdom, a man or woman may not
marry certain close relatives. Some religions prohibit
marriage between other relationships.

Blood relatives

A man may not marry his	A woman may not marry her
● mother	● father
● sister	● brother
● daughter	● son
● father's mother	● father's father
● mother's mother	● mother's father
● son's daughter	● son's son
● daughter's daughter	● daughter's son
● father's sister	● father's brother
● mother's sister	● mother's brother
● brother's daughter	● brother's son
● sister's daughter	● sister's son

Step-relatives

A man may not marry a	A woman may not marry a
● daughter of a former wife	● son of a former husband
● former wife of his father	● former husband of her mother
● former wife of his father's father	● former husband of her father's mother
● former wife of his mother's father	● former husband of her mother's mother
● daughter of a son of a former wife	● son of a son of a former husband

- daughter of a daughter of a former wife
- son of a daughter of a former husband

Relatives-in-law

A man may not marry
- the mother of a former wife
- the former wife of a son

A woman may not marry
- the father of a former husband
- the former husband of a daughter

Relations who are allowed to marry

In law certain relatives have been allowed to marry under the Marriage Act of 1986. Marriages under this Act may only take place in a civil ceremony under licence, not in church by banns.

Step-relatives

Step-relatives may marry provided that they are 21 years of age or older. The younger member of the couple must at no time, before the age of 18, have lived under the same roof as the older person. Neither must they have been treated as a child of the older person's family.

Relatives-in-law

Relatives-in-law may marry provided that they are 21 years of age or older. The former spouses (in either or both cases) must be deceased.

England and Wales

GENERAL

Marriage must take place in a district register office, in a church or chapel of the Church of England or Church of Wales, in an approved building (that is, a building

approved by the local authority under procedures
dictated by the Marriage Act 1994) or in a naval,
military or air-force chapel. The ceremony must be an
authorized civil or religious one registered by a
registrar or other authorized person and must take place
between 8 a.m. and 6 p.m. Exceptions include
marriages according to the rites and ceremonies of the
Jews or Quakers, those by Registrar General's (or
Archbishop of Canterbury's) special licence, and those
for housebound or detained persons. The marriage
must take place in front of two witnesses.

Age

In the United Kingdom, the minimum legal age for
getting married is 16. In England and Wales, the
written consent of parents or guardians is required for
people who have not yet reached 18 years of age.

CHURCH OF ENGLAND WEDDINGS

Marriage may be carried out according to the rites of
the Church of England in the following ways: by
publication of the banns; by common licence; and by
Archbishop of Canterbury's special licence.

Publishing the banns

The clergyman will arrange to have banns published in
his church for three successive Sundays. The purpose
of the banns is to make public the couple's intentions
and to invite objections to the marriage. In fact, a
church wedding is officially called 'marriage by
banns', and the three successive Sundays of
publication correspond to the 21 days in which a notice
of marriage is posted in a register office for a 'marriage
by certificate without licence'. They must be published

for each of the couple, and they are combined if the bride and groom live in the same parish.

If the groom's parish is different

When the groom comes from another parish, certain procedures have to be followed. First, the groom should approach the clergyman of his parish to inform him of the proposed wedding and the date. His clergyman will then arrange with the clergyman of the bride's church to read the banns in both churches on the same three successive Sundays. After this, he will forward a certificate, verifying that he has read the banns, to the officiating clergyman, who cannot perform the ceremony without it.

If the wedding is delayed

After all banns have been read, the marriage can take place at any time within the next three calendar months. If this time elapses, then the banns have to be read again. Banns do not have to be read immediately a date is set for the wedding. If the couple approaches their clergyman in winter to make sure of a date in summer, then the clergyman will arrange to read the banns on each of the three Sundays before the day of the wedding.

Marriage by common licence

If the couple cannot wait the 21 days for the three sets of banns to be read – due to severe illness, an imminent birth or sudden departure overseas, for example – then they may apply, through the clergyman, for a common licence, which has to be approved by the local diocesan council. Also, the licence must be applied for by a couple if one or both members are not British subjects or are not resident in England or Wales.

Requirements

The granting of the licence will depend only on one of the couple fulfilling a residential requirement in the parish of 15 days immediately prior to application. This corresponds with the requirements for a certificate and licence for a civil wedding (see pp. 40–1). Once the application has been approved, then only one clear day's notice need be given before the ceremony can take place. This has to fit in with the schedule of the clergyman in question, but the ceremony must take place within three months of the granting of the licence, otherwise a fresh application is necessary.

Marriage by special licence

Marriage by special licence is very unusual and must be approved by the Archbishop of Canterbury. Application is generally made by couples who are not British residents or who cannot marry on church premises because of circumstances, such as one party being so ill that he or she cannot leave bed. The marriage has to take place within three months of issue. Special licences also have to be issued to anyone (including royalty) wishing to marry in St Paul's Cathedral, Westminster Abbey or the chapel at Buckingham Palace. This is because none of these places is registered for marriage ceremonies to be conducted in them.

ROMAN CATHOLIC WEDDINGS

Procedures in the Roman Catholic Church are broadly similar to those of the established Churches of the United Kingdom, except that marriage is by civil preliminaries, not banns. The couple, therefore, must give notice of their intentions to the superintendent registrar of their area and follow the procedures to obtain a superintendent registrar's certificate or certificate and licence as they would for a civil ceremony (see pp. 38–41).

NONCONFORMIST WEDDINGS

Weddings in most Protestant Churches other than the Church of England follow similar procedures to the Roman Catholic Church – that is, the couple must obtain a superintendent registrar's certificate or certificate and licence to marry.

Where a particular denomination is very small – as is the case with Pentecostal sects, for example – the minister may not be authorized to register marriages, and the registrar will have to be present at the ceremony. He or she does not conduct the marriage, however, but merely records in his or her register that it has taken place.

QUAKER WEDDINGS

Six weeks prior to the wedding date, the couple must make an application to the registering officer at the Friends' monthly meeting where the marriage will take place. The couple will be given a form to take to the superintendent registrar of the area, where notice of the marriage will be posted as with civil ceremonies. Once the statutory 21 days have elapsed, the couple will be issued with the superintendent registrar's certificate which they take to the meeting house on the day of the wedding. Quakers may be married by either certificate or certificate and licence.

ORTHODOX WEDDINGS
See Roman Catholic weddings.

JEWISH WEDDINGS
Notice of the wedding needs to be given to the local
superintendent registrar, as for civil and Nonconformist
ceremonies. In most cases, however, the secretary of
the synagogue will be licensed to keep a marriage
register, so the registrar will not be required to attend to
register the wedding. It is at the couple's discretion as
to whether they marry in a synagogue or some other
place. The 8 a.m. to 6 p.m. time limit does not apply.

HINDU, MUSLIM AND SIKH WEDDINGS
The law provides for the registration of buildings such
as temples and mosques for the solemnization of
marriages according to the rites and ceremonies of
these religions. Couples should give notice of their
intention to marry and undertake civil preliminaries if
their proposed marriage is to take place in such a
building. A registrar may need to attend to register the
marriage. If a religious marriage is to take place in a
building not registered for the solemnization of
marriages, then the couple should arrange for a civil
ceremony beforehand in order to comply with
requirements of the law.

REGISTER OFFICE WEDDINGS
If the bride and groom are from different districts, they
may marry in either location depending upon their
preference. If two districts are involved, however, then
notice of intention to marry by certificate without
licence must be given in both.

Residence requirement

When marrying by certificate without licence, a couple's union may be solemnized in any register office or building approved under the procedures of the Marriage Act 1994. One of the couple must have been resident in the relevant district for a minimum of seven days prior to giving notice of intention to marry at the office concerned. Thus, one or both of the couple may have to find a residence for seven days and nights.

Establishing legality

The registrar takes personal details and establishes whether the couple may legally marry. If either or both persons are under 18, birth certificates are required. It is preferred that such evidence is produced by all persons wishing to marry. If either the prospective bride or groom has been married before, proof of how the marriage ended is needed. Depending on whether the previously married party is divorced or widowed, this would be a divorce absolute document, with the original court seal, or a death certificate or certified copy. Photocopies are not acceptable. The couple are then asked to sign a declaration that they are eligible to marry. A false declaration will not only invalidate the marriage but may render the couple liable to prosecution under the Perjury Act.

Public notice of the marriage

When the superintendent registrar is satisfied that he can take the notice of marriage, it is entered into the marriage notice book and a statutory form is displayed on a public notice board for 21 clear days. This is the equivalent of the period over which the banns are published for a Church of England marriage, and the reason is to allow anyone who has any objection to the marriage the opportunity of voicing it. The fee for posting this notice is reviewed annually in April.

Issue of the certificate of marriage

A certificate of marriage (not to be confused with the marriage certificate issued after the wedding) is then issued and held at the register office until the day of the marriage. If notice of marriage is being given in two districts, then the one issued in the other district should be collected by the bride or groom prior to the wedding, as they will be asked to produce it before the ceremony can go ahead. The marriage must take place between 21 days and three months of the date notice was given. Generally speaking, an appointment for the ceremony will be made by the couple and the superintendent registrar at that time. If a couple wish to postpone the marriage beyond the three-month period a fresh notice (or notices) of marriage will be required.

Marriage by licence

When a couple wishes to marry sooner, perhaps if there is serious illness or an imminent birth, a superintendent registrar's certificate and licence may be appropriate. Either one of the bridal couple (it does not have to be both) must have been resident in the area for 15 days prior to giving notice. If everything is in order, a licence may be issued and the marriage take place after the lapse of one clear working day following the day on which notice was entered. The notice of a marriage by certificate and licence is not posted publicly. There is an extra charge for the licence on top of the charge for the notice, payable on the day the licence is issued, or on the day of the marriage. This means two trips to the register office. The couple may then marry up to three months after the date when notice was given.

Registrar General's licence

A Registrar General's licence may only be issued when one of those wishing to marry is seriously ill, not expected to recover and cannot be removed to a place where marriages may be solemnized. The marriage may take place at any time in any place. No residence requirements are necessary. A registered medical practitioner must state in writing that the requirements of the law have been met before a Registrar General's licence may be issued.

Scotland

GENERAL

No residential qualification is required in Scotland and the bridal couple may be married in any church they wish. A minimum period of 15 days notice must be given to the registrar before the proposed date of marriage. Where a ceremony is held is at the discretion of the authorized person and the people involved. It may be at one of the couple's homes, in a hotel or in the church, although a registrar may only marry people within his office. The marriage must take place in front of two witnesses over the age of 16.

Age

The minimum legal age is 16. Parental consent is *not* required for people below the age of 18.

CHURCH WEDDINGS

Publishing the banns

Banns are no longer required in a religious ceremony.

Marriage schedule

The couple are required to submit notices of marriage to the registrar, four weeks before the proposed date (or six weeks, if either of the couple has been married before). The marriage schedule will only be issued to the couple (not more than seven days before the wedding) once the registrar is satisfied that the notices are in order. They must be given to the clergyman before the ceremony begins. Once they have been signed and witnessed, the marriage schedules have to be returned to the registrar within three days.

OTHER RELIGIOUS CEREMONIES

Whether Christian or non-Christian, notices of marriage must be given to the local registrar, and the procedures (detailed above) followed, as long as the marriage celebrants are authorized to marry people under the Marriage (Scotland) Act 1977.

REGISTER OFFICE WEDDINGS

Procedures are as above. The registrar does not issue the marriage schedule, however, but produces it at the ceremony to be signed and witnessed.

Northern Ireland

GENERAL

The residence requirement is seven days. The marriage has to take place in a building registered for the purpose – that is, a district register office or church.

Age

As for England and Wales.

RELIGIOUS AND CIVIL CEREMONIES

Notice of marriage is given to the district registrar of marriages. Marriage can take place by licence, special licence, banns, certificate from a registrar or licence from a district registrar of marriages.

Special licence

Marriages by special licence may take place anywhere at any time, at the discretion of the bishop concerned. Unless issued a special licence by a senior official of their religion, Quakers, Jews and Nonconformists require a registrar's certificate to marry. Jews do not need to marry in the district where they live.

Useful addresses

The authorities listed (below) provide information on remarriage, civil and religious, mixed-religion and interdenominational weddings, and divorce.

Baptist Union
Baptist House
129 The Broadway
Didcot
Oxon OX11 8RT
Tel.: 0235 512077

Catholic Marriage Advisory Council
Clitherow House
1 Blythe Mews
Blythe Road
London W14 0NW
Tel.: 071 371 1341

Church of Scotland
Department of
Communication
121 George Street
Edinburgh EH2 4YN
Tel.: 031 225 5722

Enquiry Centre General Synod of the Church of England
Church House
Great Smith Street
London SW1P 3NZ
Tel.: 071 222 9011

General Register Office for the Isle of Man
Finch Road
Douglas
Isle of Man
Tel.: 0624 675212

General Register Office for Northern Ireland
Oxford House
49/55 Chichester Street
Belfast BT1 4HL
Tel.: 0232 526947

General Register Office for Scotland
New Register House
Edinburgh EH1 3YT
Tel.: 031 334 0380

Jewish Marriage Council
23 Ravenshurst Avenue
London NW4 4EL
Tel.: 081 203 6311

Methodist Church Press Office
1 Central Buildings
Westminster
London SW1 9NH
Tel.: 071 222 8010

Registrar General for England and Wales
OPCS London
St Catherine's House
10 Kingsway
London WC2B 6JP
Tel.: 071 242 0262

Registrar General for Guernsey
The Greffe
Royal Court House
St Peter Port
Guernsey GY1 2PB
Tel.: 0481 725 277

Scottish Information Directory
New St Andrew's House
St James' Centre
Edinburgh EH1 3TD
Tel.: 031 556 8400

Superintendent Registrar for Jersey
States' Offices
Royal Square
St Helier
Jersey JE1 1DD
Tel.: 0534 502000

United Reformed Church
City Temple
Holborn Viaduct
London EC1A 2DE
Tel.: 071 583 8701

3. Types of wedding

The religious wedding ceremonies described in this chapter are those that are not performed according to the rites of the established Protestant Churches of the United Kingdom. Protestant Church and register office weddings are described in detail in Chapters 5 and 6. For the law and various types of religious ceremony, see Chapter 2, 'Marriage and the law', pp. 32–44.

Roman Catholic weddings

The Roman Catholic marriage service, although similar to that of Protestant Churches, includes rituals peculiar to the faith. At one time, the most marked difference was the Latin Nuptial Mass. Nowadays, with Roman Catholic ceremonies almost always conducted in the language of the host country, the differences are more subtle.

The ceremony
The bride's vows do not include the promise to obey. The ring also plays a more significant role. At the point of marriage, the groom first puts the ring on the bride's thumb, forefinger and middle finger of her left hand in sequence as he says: 'In the name of the Father, Son and Holy Ghost', before finally placing the ring on the third finger. Finally, as the bridegroom promises his bride: 'With all my worldly goods I thee endow,' he gives her some small coins as a token of this vow.

Nonconformist weddings

The ceremony
The ceremony may follow whatever rituals are
demanded by the sect, but must include, at some point,
the following declarations by both the bride and
bridegroom:

1 'I do solemnly declare that I know not of any lawful
impediment why I (full name) may not be joined in
matrimony to (full name).'
2 'I call upon these persons here present to witness
that I (full name) do take thee (full name) to be my
lawful wedded wife/husband.'

Quaker (Society of Friends) weddings

The simplest of all Christian marriages, the Quaker
wedding has no music, set order of service or sermon.
The Meeting House is unadorned, the bride and groom
wear no special dress, and there is not necessarily a
chief bridesmaid or best man.

BEFORE THE DAY
Applying to marry
If one of the bridal couple is not a Quaker, then written
support for the marriage to take place must be obtained
from two adult members of the Society. If the Friends
agree to the marriage, the registering officer will issue
the couple with a form to take to the superintendent
registrar (as is the case when both members of the

bridal couple are Quakers). Once the legalities have been dealt with (see p. 37), a notice is also given by the Quaker registering officer at the Sunday morning meeting where, if no objection is received, a date is set for the wedding to take place.

ON THE DAY
The ceremony
At the appointed time, the bride and groom pledge life-long love and loyalty to each other. A ring is not necessary as a sign of the groom's pledge to his bride; the Friends consider that his word is sufficient. However, a ring is often given at the end of the ceremony.

After the ceremony
After the marriage, the bride and groom, together with four witnesses and the registering officer, sign the civil marriage register. A lavish reception is discouraged.

Jewish weddings

The festivities surrounding a traditional Jewish wedding must be some of the most colourful of all. Certainly, anyone attending such a ceremony for the first time will be struck by the many symbolic customs involved and the joyous celebrations following the dignified official proceedings.

CUSTOMS
Jewish communities originate from many different quarters of the world – everywhere from Iran and Ethiopia to Germany and Russia, Spain and the Yemen. It is therefore not suprising that the customs vary

considerably in detail, although certain basic
procedures are constant. Customs vary somewhat, too,
according to the degree of orthodoxy. The Reform and
Liberal movements, for example, are far less traditional
in their approach than the Lubavitch, a sect who dress,
even in the late 20th century, in the garb of their
forefathers from Eastern Europe. Lubavitch brides, for
example, cut their hair short prior to marriage and don a
wig or *scheitel*, so that the beauty of their natural hair is
for a husband's eyes only.

BEFORE THE DAY
Setting the date
The wedding is fixed on a day that is accepted by
Jewish law. Weddings are not permitted to coincide
with certain festivals, for instance, nor may they take
place on the Sabbath.
Symbolic cleansing ceremony
The bride and groom do not usually see each other for
at least a day prior to their marriage. Also, shortly
before her wedding day, the traditional Jewish bride
visits what is known as the *mikveh*. This is a ritual bath
house. Here, she completely immerses herself in a
symbolic cleansing ceremony. Most established Jewish
communities have a *mikveh* somewhere in their
communal buildings.

ON THE DAY
Where the ceremony takes place
Not all Jewish weddings take place in a synagogue as
might be expected, for rabbinical law provides that they
may take place almost anywhere, even outdoors,
providing the actual ceremony is conducted under a

canopy, known as the *chuppah*. Quite commonly, this will be decorated with flowers, and it may be held by special attendants or be fixed in position.

Wedding clothes

There are no fixed rules about how the couple should dress, but it is customary for the bride to wear white as a sign of purity, and to have a headress and a veil. Extremely orthodox Jewish grooms may don a *kittel* or long white robe, but this is not widely worn. Oriental brides frequently wear quite elaborate costumes and jewellery.

The ceremony

The Jewish marriage contract, or *ketubah*, is signed during the ceremony and duly witnessed. Before this, the groom will have been led to the bride, checking that she is indeed his intended before the veil is let down over her face. The groom will usually be led into the ceremony by his own and the bride's father, while the bride is led by her own mother and that of the groom. In some communities, it is then customary for the bride to make seven circuits around the groom. Some believe that this ceremony is performed to ward off evil spirits.

Consecration of the bride

Benedictions are recited under the canopy, where the couple's parents stand. The groom will duly place a ring on the forefinger of the bride's right hand and recite, in Hebrew 'Behold, you are consecrated unto me by this ring, according to the law of Moses and of Israel.' The bride and groom are also both given wine to drink from a goblet.

Conclusion of the ceremony

In many communities, at the conclusion of the

ceremony, a glass is crushed underfoot by the groom, while the congregants shout 'Mazzeltov!' (meaning 'Good luck and congratulations!'). Most authorities consider this tradition to be a mark, even on such a joyous occasion, of the destruction of the Temple and of the need to remember that others are perhaps not so fortunate as oneself. The traditional festivities – often involving much feasting, singing and dancing (men and women separately in the more orthodox communities) – can now begin!

Non-Jewish guests

If, as a Jew, you are planning a traditional wedding that will be conducted by a rabbi, it may be as well to provide some *kippot* or skullcaps for non-Jewish men who might arrive without the required head covering. When attending a synagogue, it is customary for women who are married also to cover their heads. Arms should also generally be covered, although not all communities are so strict about this.

The reception

At the ensuing celebrations, the meal is not started until someone has said a blessing over bread. The meal also concludes with Grace and seven special benedictions, sung in Hebrew.

**Jewish wedding ceremony
under a *chuppah*** (right)
1 Groom's parents   4 Bride
2 Groom   5 Bride's parents
3 Rabbi

Greek Orthodox weddings

The ceremony

Weddings in the Greek Orthodox community basically follow the traditional Christian ceremony but certain specific customs are observed. Linked crowns are placed on the couple's heads as a sign of their unity, and very many witnesses will record their presence at the ceremony. The service may be conducted both in Greek and in the language of the host country, and much of it will be chanted.

The reception

But perhaps the most familiar custom of all takes place at the reception, when the bride and groom will have paper money of any denomination at all pinned to their outfits. At wealthy gatherings, this could easily total several thousands of pounds. What a wonderful start in practical terms to their future together!

Muslim weddings

BEFORE THE DAY

Arranging the marriage

Many Muslim weddings are arranged between two families, with the bride and groom having limited choice of partner. However, they do have the opportunity of rejecting a marriage proposed in this way, and most families respect these wishes.

The preparations

When everything has been agreed, the preparations for the marriage begin. Families play an important part in these preparations – the bride and groom rarely do it themselves.

Pre-wedding parties

In the week before the wedding, two parties take place, first at the groom's and then at the bride's home. These are for the families and close friends of the bride and groom, respectively, to offer gifts to the other family as well as to the bridal couple. Also offered at both parties is *mehndi* – a mixture of henna leaves and water – which is used to paint the bride's and groom's hands on the day of the marriage.

ON THE DAY
Wedding clothes

On the morning of the wedding, the bride and groom are dressed by close members of their families – always of the same sex. The groom is dressed in white and puts on a special hat called a *kula*. In some communities, the bride is dressed in her colourful bridal robes, usually red with gold-thread embroidery, and intricate patterns are painted on her hands with *mehndi*. She is heavily veiled because Islam dictates that the groom does not see her face (on the day) until after the ceremony.

Just before the ceremony

The groom is attended throughout the wedding by a *serbala*, the youngest boy in the family, usually a sister's son. He is dressed in white and also wears a *kula*. The family give gifts of money – *salami* – to the groom for good luck. He and the *serbala* are then fed *laddu*, a sweet food made from chickpeas, sugar and butter, immediately before departing for the marriage ceremony.

The ceremony
The marriage usually takes place at the bride's home,
where the groom and *serbala* are given garlands in
welcome. The marriage is conducted by an imam, who
reads from the Koran. The bride and groom sit
separately during their marriage, possibly on opposite
sides of the room. The bride's father and two witnesses
ask the bride if she has agreed to the marriage, after
which the imam asks the groom if he has agreed. After
both agree, the imam completes the *nikahnama* – the
Muslim marriage certificate.

After the ceremony
A magnificent meal follows, but the bride and groom
are still separated, sitting with their respective families.
Then the bride leaves to prepare to be presented to her
husband. She puts on all the jewellery she has been
given for the wedding. At last, she comes to sit next to
the groom and her veil is lifted for him to see her face.

Preparing for the wedding night
They then travel together to the groom's house where
they are fed *laddu* in welcome. The bride is taken up to
see her new bedroom. First, she has to cut a red garland
which has been placed across the doorway. Inside, her
sister or a close female relative helps her take off her
shoes and rest, and prepare for her wedding night.

AFTER THE DAY
The civil ceremony
A few days later, a second marriage, a civil ceremony,
may take place. This is required if the mosque is not
registered for the solemnization of marriages.
Otherwise, previous to the religious ceremony, the

couple are required to undertake civil preliminaries
(see 'Marriage and the law, pp. 38 and 42).

The reception
After the civil ceremony, the wedding party returns to
the bride's house for the *valeema* – the main wedding
reception, in which both the bride's and groom's
relatives and friends feast and offer more gifts to the
newlyweds.

Hindu weddings

Marriage is one of a series of holy sacraments in the
Hindu religion, just as it is in the Roman Catholic
Church. Hindus believe marriage has a purifying
quality, and attach a great deal of religious and social
significance to it.

BEFORE THE DAY
Arranging the marriage
Hindu marriages are normally arranged between two
families on the assumption that those already united in
marriage know best what will lead to a happy marriage
for their children. As astrology is important in the
Hindu religion, a bridal couple's horoscopes will be
charted to test for compatibility. While the individuals
concerned have the right to refuse the match, usually
they trust their families to make the right choice. The
marriage is often finally agreed at a dinner party with
six men from each family present. The bride and
groom do not see each other alone prior to the wedding
day.

Choosing the date and pre-wedding parties
The date of the marriage ceremony is decided by the

priest, who consults each of the couple's horoscope to
choose the most suitable day. Weeks of preparation
follow, during which a party is held at the groom's
house, where gifts between the families are exchanged
and sweet foods and money are offered to the groom.
The bride and her family have their own party, where
she is offered sweet foods and has her hands painted
with red henna dye. The groom's relatives send the
bride jewellery and money, but it is customary for the
bride's family to pay for the wedding.

The night before the wedding
On the eve of the wedding, both the bride and the
groom say prayers to Ganesha, the elephant god of
plenty, usually in their own homes.

ON THE DAY
Wedding clothes
On the day, the bride is assisted by her close female
relatives in bathing and the painting of intricate patterns
on her hands and feet with red henna dye. Her bridal
sari is a single piece of cloth and is usually red with
complicated patterns embroidered in gold thread. She is
also adorned with the costly Indian 24-carat gold
jewellery given to her by the groom's family.

Where the ceremony takes place
The Hindu marriage celebration is a colourful occasion.
It can take place in the temple where the bride
worships, which is highly decorated and probably
boasts many ornate sculptures. Often, however, the
marriage takes place in the bride's home, which is
decorated specially for the event.

Just before the ceremony

As the time of the ceremony draws near the groom, dressed in traditional Indian white trousers, tunic and ceremonial hat, and his relatives are welcomed at the bride's home with garlands. He is led into the marriage room where the father of the bride offers him gifts. After this welcome, his bride enters the room and sits facing him under a richly decorated canopy, called a *mandaps*. In some ceremonies, both are heavily veiled until they are married.

The ceremony

The marriage is performed by a Hindu priest, who begins with prayers. Music is often played on the *sehnai*, an Indian version of the oboe. After words emphasizing the importance of marriage, and statements of good intent from the bride and groom, the priest ties the couple's right hands together with cord and sprinkles holy water over them. At this point, the bride's father gives his daughter to the groom. The sacred *arti* flame is then lit and the couple make an offering of rice to symbolize their hope of fertility. The bride then touches a sacred stone, and prayers are offered that its firmness will pass to her.

The Seven Steps

The most important part of the ceremony is the Seven Steps – the couple are not husband and wife until this rite has been completed. The bride and groom together either take seven steps around the fire or walk around it seven times. The Seven Steps denote food, strength, wealth, fortune, children, happy seasons and friendships. In some variations of the ceremony, the groom presents his new wife with a new sari and she

changes to symbolize her new status in her new family.
Ceremonial eating, prayers and readings
The newlyweds then feed each other five times with
morsels of sweet food, which is first offered to the
household god, as is customary with all food. The
ceremony ends with prayers and readings, and the
wedding party retires to another room where feasting
and celebrations get under way. This can last for several
days, with hundreds of relatives and friends visiting the
house to offer their gifts and congratulations.

AFTER THE DAY
The civil ceremony
A civil ceremony may be required by law (see pp. 38
and 42). As the procedures and requirements for the
civil and religious ceremonies are completely separate,
it is possible for the civil marriage to take place first.
However, in the eyes of their families and the Hindu
community, the couple are only properly married after
the religious ceremony has been performed. Until then,
they are deemed unmarried and may not meet alone.

Sikh weddings

Sikhs have many customs in common with both the
Hindu and Muslim religions, which include the
marriage ceremony. The choice of marriage partner is
made with help and advice from both families; the
couple are allowed to meet before the marriage but
always with other people present. The most important
requirement for the prospective marriage partners is
that both are Sikhs.

BEFORE THE DAY
Pre-wedding parties
As with Muslim and Hindu weddings, parties are held in both the bride's and the groom's houses, where gifts are exchanged, with the strict proviso that the Guru Granth Sahib – the Sikh holy book – is present.

The bride's preparations
Customs differ from family to family, depending on the region in the Punjab, India, from which they originally came. In some families, five of the bride's close relatives – the nearest equivalent to bridesmaids – stay with the bride all the time in the days leading up to the wedding. They look after her and, on the eve of the wedding, perform the ritual of combing a mixture of henna, oil and water through her hair. This is meant to downgrade her looks, so that on the morning of her wedding, she becomes beautiful for her husband after the ritual bathing.

ON THE DAY
Wedding clothes
For her marriage, the bride wears either red trousers, *shalwar*, and tunic, *kameez*, or a red sari made from a single piece of cloth, and a red headscarf, *chunni*. She is adorned with the jewellery given by the groom's family. She also wears a heavy veil which is not lifted until she is married. The groom may wear either Western dress or traditional Eastern white clothes, but he must wear a scarf and his turban.

Where the ceremony takes place
The marriage ceremony itself usually takes place in the *gurdwara*, the Sikh place of worship, but this is not

compulsory. Often the ceremony is held in the bride's home. Wherever it takes place, the Guru Granth Sahib must be present.

The ceremony

Any Sikh may be in charge of the ceremony, as long as both families agree. Often it is the *granthi*, or holy man. The ceremony begins with an explanation of the importance of marriage. The couple show they agree to be married by bowing to the Guru Granth Sahib. Then the bride's father ties the bride's chunni to the groom's scarf to symbolize her departure to join the groom's family.

Walking around the Guru Granth Sahib

A marriage hymn of four verses, the 'Lavan', written by the Sikh teacher Guru Ram Das, is then sung. To symbolize their support, relatives help the bridal couple to walk around the Guru Granth Sahib after each verse of the hymn has been sung. When they have walked round four times, they are married. Throughout the ceremony, hymns are sung and prayers are said for the future happiness of the newlyweds.

Final prayers and ceremonial eating

Final prayers are then said and sweet food *karah parshad*, made from flour and sugar, is shared by everyone as symbolic of God's blessing on the marriage. A meal follows, either at the temple if the ceremony has taken place there – the food will have been prepared by the bride's female relatives – or at the bride's home.

The civil ceremony

A civil marriage, too, may be required to legalize the union (see 'Marriage and the law', pp. 38 and 42).

Customs and superstitions

OMENS, GOOD AND BAD

Many objects, people and even animals feature in
wedding-day superstitions; they have special powers
associated with them, especially if they are passed by
on the way to the wedding.

Good luck omens include seeing a lamb, toad, spider,
black cat or dove, or meeting a chimney sweep. Omens
of bad luck include seeing a pig or funeral, or hearing a
cock crow after dawn.

Rain is considered to be a sign of bad luck in some
cultures ('Happy the bride whom the sun shines on')
and good luck in others. Snow can indicate fertility and
prosperity, but cloudy skies or wind could augur
problems between the newly married couple.

The custom of secrecy

Transporting the bride in secret to the wedding
ceremony is a custom found, in varying forms, in
several cultures. In traditional Chinese weddings, the
bride was carried in a covered sedan chair. The bridal
veil used as a disguise dates back to Roman times.
Today, the veil is worn in only the most formal
weddings, and many brides choose to hire a special
wedding limousine or vintage car for going to and from
the ceremony. The tradition of secrecy is still
maintained in the well-worn superstition that it is bad
luck for the groom to see the bride's dress before the
wedding or to see the bride before the ceremony.
Jewish tradition has no such superstitious custom,
although bridal veils do feature in some Jewish
weddings as part of a pre-wedding ceremony in which

Wedding day omens

Omens of good luck

lamb

toad

spider

black cat

dove

chimney sweep

Omens of bad luck

pig

funeral

cock crowing
after dawn

the groom places the veil over the bride's face after checking to ensure that she is his intended bride.

Ring ceremonies

Many types of wedding service include a ring ceremony of some kind. Most of these ring ceremonies involve the groom placing a ring on the bride's ring finger, or the bride and groom exchanging rings. The ring finger is most often the third finger of the left hand; one tradition claims that a sensitive vein or nerve runs from the heart to this finger. Whereas the engagement ring is a sign of possession, the wedding ring is a symbol of unity and harmony. Jewish law holds that the exchange of the ring is so significant that it legalizes the marriage, even in the event that the ceremony has not yet finished.

The wedding ceremony, in most cultures, contains many such symbols of the new union and the couple's new status. Although they go to great pains to remain separate up to the marriage ceremony itself, couples symbolize their union by leaving the wedding together. In traditional Jewish and some Hindu wedding ceremonies, a glass is broken as a symbol of the consummation of the marriage (see p. 50). It is also thought to ward off evil spirits.

The sacred union may also be symbolized by joining hands or tying the clothes of the bride and groom together.

In a wedding tradition practised in Burma, the groom must actually pass through a cloth barrier, after paying money to the bride's family and friends, before he can be united with his bride.

AFTER THE CEREMONY
Leaving the church
The wedding party may emerge from the church under
a guard of honour of ceremonial swords – particularly
appropriate if either of the couple have military
connections – a canopy of ribbons, or to a reception in
keeping with their hobbies and interests. This could be
a football, hockey or cricket team in suitable sporting
attire, or a party of schoolchildren if one of the newly
married couples is a schoolteacher.

Bells are often also rung as the couple leave the church,
which is the traditional way of announcing to the whole
town or village that a wedding has just taken place.
Confetti
Throwing confetti (or other small, harmless items) after
the wedding ceremony has ancient roots and takes
many different forms in various cultures. In Ancient
Rome, nuts were tossed by the bridegroom after the
ceremony; in Britain, couples used to be showered with
real flowers or their petals. The word 'confetti' is
Italian for sweets, which are used in modern-day Italy.
Raisins, nuts and sweet cakes can also symbolise the
well-wishers' hopes that the couple will enjoy a sweet
and 'fruitful' marriage. Rice and grain are other forms
of 'confetti' symbolizing prosperity and fertility.
Shoes
Like confetti, shoes play a part in post-wedding
customs in bestowing good luck for the future; at one
time, they too were thrown at the newlyweds! Today,
they are more likely to be tied to the back of the
newlyweds' car. If a father gives a pair of his
daughter's shoes to her new husband, custom would

have it that he is passing on responsibility for her to his son-in-law. Another custom claims that if the son-in-law taps his new wife on the forehead with one of the shoes, he is asserting his domination of her. Fortunately, this custom now seems to have fallen completely out of favour.

Tossing the bouquet

Throwing the bridal bouquet is a fairly recent addition to the wedding rituals. All the bridesmaids (or, as is more common today, all unmarried female guests) assemble in readiness, and the bride (sometimes with her back turned so as not to direct it at anyone intentionally) tosses the bouquet. The woman who catches it is supposedly the next to 'catch' a husband.

Crossing the threshhold

Carrying the bride over the threshold of the newlyweds' home may harken back to the days when men stole off with their reluctant brides. According to another tradition, it is a way to ensure good luck. Yet another claims it prevents the bride from stepping into her new home left foot first, which is meant to bring bad luck to the couple. A similar tradition, that the bride must not touch the threshold when entering her new home, is upheld in Hindu weddings.

It is also said that, once married, the first one of the couple to purchase a new item will be the dominating partner; one tradition holds that, to ensure she is the lucky one, the bride should have her attendant, or chief bridesmaid, carry a small item, such as a pin, which can be purchased immediately following the wedding.

4. Alternative weddings

Although by far the most common form of marriage ceremony is that performed according to the rites of the Church of England, several alternatives are available to couples who, by virtue of their circumstances, marital status (divorced, for example), religion, or even preference, are looking for something different. Whatever the choice, however, it must satisfy the demands of civil law.

Military weddings

If either of the couple (or both) is a member of the armed services, then they can choose to be married in uniform instead of the traditional white dress for the bride and formal suit for the groom. The ceremony can also take place on service property licensed for marriages. Either the regulation uniform or a dress version (if permitted)) would be appropriate. Guests or other attendants – if they are military personnel – can also wear uniform.

GUARD OF HONOUR

The most striking difference between a civilian and military wedding is the guard of honour, which is composed entirely of military personnel, using drawn military swords to make a canopy for the bridal couple as they emerge from the church. If either of the couple is serving with a Scottish regiment, then a second guard of honour playing the regimental tune on the bagpipes lends a special note to the occasion.

A guard of honour

MARRIAGE ON SERVICE PROPERTY

Marriage on service property, which is not licensed for marriages (such as an aircraft hangar or a ship), is not permitted.

Marrying abroad

If a couple wishes to marry outside England and Wales or Scotland – perhaps one or both has established a life in another country, or one is a national of the host country – then they must satisfy the laws of that country and follow its customs and procedures. To find out what these are, the embassy or consulate of the country involved will have the answers to most questions, including eligibility.

LEGAL REQUIREMENTS

Most countries will almost certainly require each of the couple to produce evidence of eligibility to marry, which will include: a birth certificate; passports or other confirmation of domicility; evidence of single status (if either has been married before, the death certificate of a dead spouse or a certified copy of a decree absolute in cases of divorce); proof that neither has a current criminal conviction; and, possibly, authorized evidence of good health (the United States, for example, requires a couple to take a blood test before a marriage can take place).

Recognition in the United Kingdom

Marriages contracted according to the law of a foreign country will normally be recognized in the United Kingdom, provided the laws governing marriage and eligibility in the United Kingdom are not contravened.

For example, the marriage must be monogamous. The couple should make thorough investigations prior to the marriage. The British Embassy or Consulate in the country involved should be advised of the marriage in any case, and will be able to establish whether or not the marriage is valid in the United Kingdom. Otherwise, if there is some impediment to recognition in the United Kingdom, then the couple may have to go to court for a decision, which may not go in their favour.

Double weddings

Although unusual by virtue of two close couples deciding to marry at the same time, the double wedding is a perfect occasion for an out-of-the-ordinary celebration.

REASONS FOR A DOUBLE WEDDING

The common reason for having a double wedding is when sisters or brothers are thinking of getting married at about the same time. The guests would be largely the same if the weddings were held separately. This may also hold for a double wedding involving cousins, except for extra guests from the in-law sides.

ADVANTAGES

A double wedding may save substantially on costs, particularly of the reception – couples who opt for a double wedding may pool resources and choose a more lavish wedding and reception than each could have afforded on their own.

POSSIBLE PROBLEMS
The number of guests
Double weddings involving close friends would mean
inviting guests from four different families (and four
sets of friends) which might make the proceedings
unwieldy or mean cutting individual guest lists
drastically in order to contain numbers.

Lack of space
However, before going ahead with peripheral
arrangements, the couples should check with the
minister of their chosen church, or with the
Superintendent Registrar in the case of a register office
ceremony, that there are no objections to the event.
There are no legal impediments, but the buildings just
may not be large enough to accommodate all those who
may be attending.

SEPARATE AND JOINT ARRANGEMENTS
Apart from these considerations, the couples should
proceed in making the legal arrangements for their
marriage separately, teaming up only for organizing the
brides', grooms' and attendants' dress, the reception,
order of precedence – whose car will arrive first, whose
best man will act as toastmaster, etc. – and invitations.

Second weddings

IF EITHER PARTNER IS DIVORCED
Register office
Marriage the second time round, for either or both
partners, in front of a superintendent registrar should
present no problems if evidence of single status can be
proved, and divorce has been conducted legally.

The Church of England

A church wedding, however, is a different matter, and needs careful consideration. The Church of England used to forbid outright the marriage of divorced persons in its churches, and many vicars will still not entertain the idea. However, some are sympathetic, especially if the divorced partner is the innocent party, but the decision to marry the couple will almost certainly rest with the bishop of the diocese to which the particular church belongs. The couple should consult the clergyman of the chosen church before making plans.

Nonconformists

Many free churches – Methodist, Baptist, United Reformed – take a more modern view, and will permit even the guilty party in a divorce to remarry in their churches. The couple should approach the clergyman of their choice, as the decision will rest with him.

Quakers

A Quaker contemplating a second marriage must put his or her circumstances before the monthly Meeting for the members to decide whether he or she might be married again in front of the Meeting. Without their permission, the marriage cannot take place.

The Roman Catholic Church

The Roman Catholic Church will marry a divorced person if the previous marriage was solely a civil ceremony, as this is not recognized by the Church. Where the previous marriage was contracted before a priest, the Church does not recognize the right of the State to dissolve a marriage through divorce, and will not marry a person with a partner still living.

In some circumstances, however, the Roman Catholic Church will not recognize a previous religious ceremony – if, for example, it was conducted outside its authority, possibly in a church of another denomination. A couple should consult their clergyman with regard to the possibility of petitioning the Church to have a previous marriage declared null and void. There is a special Marriage Tribunal in the Roman Catholic Church which has this power, and the dispensation of annulment comes from the Pope.

Church of Scotland

Officially, the remarriage of divorced people is allowed under the auspices of the Church of Scotland. Very often, though, such a marriage would take place only at the discretion of the minister concerned.

IF THE FIRST SPOUSE IS DECEASED

There is no legal or ecclesiastical problem anywhere if either of the couple is widowed. However, a widow might feel it is inappropriate to be married in formal white dress with full regalia although, if she is a first-time bride marrying a widower, she may consider this to be perfectly in order.

SERVICE OF BLESSING

Where the bride and groom find that permission for their second marriage, whatever the church, is going to be difficult to obtain, they may opt for a civil ceremony and ask the minister of their particular denomination to conduct a service of blessing for the marriage. Most will agree, but the couple should remember that a blessing is not an alternative to a marriage ceremony.

SENSITIVE ISSUES
The ring
A woman getting married for the second time usually does not expect her first wedding ring to be used again (if she still has it), although there is no law against this.
Wedding guests
Very careful consideration will need to be given as to who should be invited to any reception. The chances are that it will be a more modest affair than for a first wedding reception. Indeed, in order not to risk offence, it may be best to keep the guest list to an absolute minimum and to make the reasons for this known.

Interdenominational weddings

In stricter times, the only way for partners of different denominations to marry in church was for one to convert to the other's denomination. This is not necessarily the case nowadays.

ROMAN CATHOLIC CHURCH
This used to be particularly true of the Roman Catholic Church. Conversion involved lengthy tutelage in the rites of the Church, followed by a ceremony of acceptance. Today, although the Church does not insist on conversion, the clergyman will ask for a signed statement that the children of the marriage will be brought up in the faith before he will agree to perform the ceremony.
Roman Catholic Nuptial Mass
If the ceremony is to be held in a Roman Catholic church, and the bride and groom want the Nuptial Mass, then they should establish with the clergyman

who is eligible to take the communion. Very likely it
will be available only to Roman Catholics. If so, the
couple must make the choice of either having half the
wedding party take communion, while the other half
sits and waits (the Nuptial mass can take up to half-an-
hour), or of dispensing with that part of the service
altogether.

INFORMING THE CLERGYMEN

Before the bride and groom arrange their wedding, the
ministers of both denominations have to be informed in
the same way that clergymen of the same denomination
do when the bride and groom live in different parishes.
Banns should be read in both churches (if applicable).
Some ministers are willing to co-officiate in the
marriage ceremony.

Mixed-religion weddings

It is by no means unusual today for a bride and groom
to follow completely different religions. It may be
possible to have a service which incorporates both
traditions, but the couple should seek advice from a
clergyman of each religion before making any plans. It
may be necessary, though, for one or other partner to
change religions to gain permission to marry. If the
church of their choice will not marry them without
conversion, then it may be better to have a civil
ceremony and a service of blessing afterwards. This is
often the route taken where one partner is Hindu, Sikh
or Muslim. Then, respective religious traditions and
customs can be observed without causing upset with
regard to the validity of the marriage.

Weddings at home

The obvious appeal of having your wedding at home is that you can lend a great sense of intimacy to the proceedings while eliminating the more impersonal, and probably more costly, elements of a formal church or register office ceremony. Professional advice and/or practical help can be called in whenever you think necessary, but you may find you have both the time and the inclination to do most of the work yourself.

Where home weddings are allowed

Remember that it is only possible to have a legally-binding ceremony at your own home if you live in certain countries – the United States, for example – although there is nothing to stop you arranging for the wedding reception to take place in your own home wherever you may live.

In both England and Wales it is illegal to get married anywhere other than in 'a place of worship', or in a register office. The exceptions to this rule are a military establishment which is licensed for marriages or, in the event that either party was seriously ill, then it is also permissable for a registrar to perform the ceremony either in hospital or at the bedside.

In certain circumstances it may also be possible to arrange for a private 'blessing' of the union at home as long as it follows a civil ceremony recognized by law. In Scotland, however, while the same restrictions apply to the registrar, it is possible for a recognized clergyman to conduct a legally-binding ceremony anywhere – at a person's home, for example – as long as they are able and willing to do so.

Weddings at sea

The law limits the possibilities for those who have long
harboured a desire to be married on board a ship.
Contrary to popular myth, a ship's captain is not
permitted by law in England, Wales or Scotland to
marry a couple either on land or sea. Such a marriage
would be considered a civil ceremony and must be
conducted by a registered official in a place sanctioned
for marriage by law. (For more information on the legal
requirements in relation to setting and celebrant, see
Chapter 2, 'Marriage and the Law'.)

Posting the notice of marriage

If one of the parties to a marriage is a serving member
of the Royal Navy (under the Naval Marriages Act,
1908), the commanding officer (or ship's chaplain)
may post the notice of marriage by civil ceremony – or
publish the banns – on board ship in the same way that
the superintendent registrar and the minister of religion
do so on land. The chaplain or commanding officer
may also issue the necessary certificate after the
necessary 21 days have elapsed. This concession,
however, does not apply to members of either the
public or the Merchant Navy.

Celebration

Of course, couples are always free to hold their
reception, or any other wedding celebrations, at sea as
long as their actual wedding conforms to the legal
requirements. Some couples may even want to hold a
duplicate ceremony on board ship following a civil
ceremony.

Older partners

There is no difference in the legal requirements for a
couple marrying late in life and for the first time, but
they themselves may wish to modify the trappings of
the traditional ceremony. The bride, for example, may
feel she is too old to wear a long, formal white dress.
Most such styles are designed for women in their late
teens, twenties and thirties, the most common ages for
women to marry for the first time. Therefore, the older
bride may prefer to choose a special day dress in a
flattering colour for herself and her attendants.

Paying for the wedding

Instead of having the bride's parents host the occasion
(or at least share the costs with the groom's parents) –
as is common in the more traditional weddings – an
older couple may wish to bear the cost of the wedding
themselves. They will probably be established in their
careers and lifestyles, unlike most younger couples
who are just starting out. In addition, the couple's
parents may be elderly and on a pension, or they may
no longer even be alive.

Gretna Green weddings

In times gone by, when all else failed, a young couple
from England or Wales whose parents had refused
consent for them to be married had recourse to Gretna
Green, in Scotland. These northern weddings began in
the 1700s with an act of Parliament allowing Scotland
to avoid new strict laws governing marriage in England
and Wales. At first, desperate couples flocked to

Edinburgh to be married, but logic supported the
establishment of a wedding site closer to the border;
thus Gretna Green, a town right on the English/Scottish
border, gained in popularity for those escaping parental
disapproval.

The situation today
Since the Marriage (Scotland) Act of 1939 came into
force on 1 July 1940, couples have had to fulfil a
residency requirement and prove eligibility in a way
that is similar to the procedure in England and Wales.
Scottish law, however, still allows anyone over the age
of 16 to marry without parental consent, whereas in
England and Wales, young couples must wait until the
age of majority (currently 18) for this freedom.

Homosexual weddings

In certain communities, such as San Francisco in the
United States, it is possible to go through a form of
homosexual 'marriage'. As the whole concept is fairly
new, there are no strict rules or traditions which need to
be followed. The legality of the ceremony also remains
questionable.

5. Register office weddings

RELIGIOUS AND CIVIL CEREMONIES
In the United Kingdom, the fundamental difference
between getting married in a church and in a register
office is that the latter has no religious significance. A
marriage is first and foremost a civil ceremony. It has to
be recognized by law and performed by a registered
marriage celebrant.

Reasons for a civil ceremony
There are many reasons why a couple might opt to be
married in a register office.

Religious reasons
Perhaps a religious ceremony has been discouraged or,
indeed, forbidden by the clergymen that the couple
have approached. Some are quite strict. Examples of
why they may decline to marry certain people are given
below.

Religious impediments
● If the partners are of differing religions
● If either or both partners are divorced
● If a couple does not regularly attend the place of
  worship

Unlike a clergyman, however, a superintendent registrar
has no power to refuse to marry a couple unless there is
a legal impediment.

Legal reasons
Some religious marriage ceremonies are not legally

recognized – for example, those of the Hindu or Sikh
religions. So couples professing such faiths are
required to marry according to civil law (see 'Marriage
and the law', pp. 32–44), if they wish their marriage to
have legal recognition.

Other reasons

Very often, though, it is the couple who decide against
a church wedding. If they have no firm religious
beliefs, they may view being married in church as
hypocritical, and will regard vows made in front of a
superintendent registrar as being just as valid as any
made at the altar.

Before the day

CHOOSING A REGISTER OFFICE

As with a church wedding, it is usual for the marriage
to take place near the bride's home. Unless the town is
very large, there will be only one register office nearby.
It is a civic department, combined with the registry of
births and deaths, and is usually to be found in the
Town Hall or other municipal building. The bridal
couple should check the hours that the superintendent
regsistrar is in attendance before setting a date for the
marriage. Not all offices work full time, and it would
cause unnecessary inconvenience if wedding plans
have been made for a date when the office is closed.

Residence requirements

If the bride and groom come from completely different
towns, either location would be suitable, depending on
the couple's preference (see 'Marriage and the law',
pp. 39 and 41).

THE INTERVIEW

Having made the decision to marry in a register office,
the couple should first make an appointment to see the
superintendent registrar at the office of their choice.
Both need not attend, but the one that does go will need
to know all the information about the other person that
the registrar requires. It is easier, therefore, if both can
attend, as this will avoid having to make another
appointment because some facts remain unknown. The
procedure that follows is similar to that when seeing a
clergyman about a church wedding (see pp. 89-105).

Marriageability and types of authorization

During the interview, the superintendent registrar will
ascertain whether both of the couple are eligible to
marry and whether they wish the marriage to be
authorized by superintendent registrar's certificate,
certificate and licence or Registrar General's licence.
For details about types of authorization, see 'Marriage
and the law', pp. 39–41 and 42. At this stage, the
superintendent registrar will post the marriage notice
for which he or she will require payment.

SIZE OF THE OFFICE

When booking the date for their wedding, the couple
should ask to see the room where the ceremony will
take place. Some register offices have more than one
room. In many cases, an effort is made to make them
look special with attractive decorations, soft
furnishings and flowers. The rooms, however, are far
smaller than the average-sized church, possibly only
holding 30 people, including the bridal party. While
under the Marriage Act, the registrar must conduct the

ceremony 'with open doors' (that is, he or she cannot prevent anyone who wants to witness the marriage from doing so), it would make a farce of the proceedings if too many guests were to cram into a room which would not accommodate them. So the couple should not expect their wedding to be witnessed by hundreds of relatives and friends.

NUMBER OF GUESTS

The couple will need to ask how many people may be accommodated comfortably in the room, and plan their invitations accordingly. Choosing who can physically attend the ceremony may be difficult but it will avoid embarrassment on the day.

Choosing who should attend

With a large family, for example, it may be wiser not to have attendants so that more relatives may be invited. Another way to solve the problem is to invite all the other guests to share in the celebration at the reception afterwards. Most people will understand the pressure on space in a register office and will not take offence.

Inviting guests to the reception

It is important that invitations to the reception only state very clearly that this is the case. By omitting the time and place of the ceremony, any confusion should be avoided. An example of an invitation to the reception, which cannot be misinterpreted as an invitation to the ceremony, is given opposite.

WITNESSES

The bridal couple should then decide who will 'witness' their marriage. The law demands only two people to be present and to sign the register afterwards.

Witnesses may be anyone – even total strangers – but couples usually choose friends or relatives. The best man and bride's father are conventional choices, but a bridesmaid would be equally acceptable. Otherwise, arrangements can proceed in the same way as for a church wedding.

Invitation to a reception

Mr and Mrs John Jackson
request the pleasure of the presence of

Mr and Mrs Robin Fisher
at the reception following the wedding of their daughter
Jacqueline
to
Mr William Barclay

Please come to Woolton Hall, High St, Woolton
at 3 p.m. on Saturday, 22 April 1993.

RSVP by 24 March 1993   99 Churchfield Road,
                               Liverpool 25
                               Tel: 051-428 4675

On the day

BEFORE THE CEREMONY

On the day itself, the wedding party should arrive at the register office in good time for the start of the ceremony. The groom may arrive first, as tradition demands, but the bride does not have the 'privilege' of arriving late. Register offices are more tied to time than

The register office ceremony

Who may be present at the ceremony (right)

The number of people attending a registry office wedding is limited only by the size of the space available. Most couples keep their guest list to a minimum, yet invite additional guests to a reception following the ceremony. Although the exact arrangement of the room varies from one registry office to another, most contain the registrar's table, or podium, and rows of chairs on either side to accommodate friends and relatives. Alternatively, chairs may be placed in rows facing the registrar, thereby allowing friends and family to mingle.

A typical ceremony arrangement is shown in the illustration (right).

The procedure

The actual ceremony takes only 10-20 minutes. After the vows have been made and the rings exchanged (if the couple have chosen to do so), the bride and groom sign the register first, followed by the two witnesses. Finally, the registrar and superintendent registrar sign, so completing the procedure.

1 Registrar
2 Groom
3 Bride
4 First witness (eg best man)
5 Second witness (eg bridesmaid)
6 Friends and members of bride's family
7 Friends and members of groom's family

churches, performing marriage ceremonies constantly
throughout the day.

Private interview with the registrar

The superintendent registrar, with whom the couple has
dealt over the previous weeks, is in attendance during
the ceremony. A registrar, however, conducts the
wedding and, at the appointed time, he or she calls the
names of the bride and groom for a private interview.
This is to check that the information given in the first
interview is still correct, and to collect the fee for his or
her attendance, and to make entry of the marriage into
the register and one copy of the marriage certificate.
The rest of the wedding party may then enter. The
couple and the witnesses approach the table where the
registrar waits to perform the ceremony, while the
wedding party may sit behind on chairs provided.
Otherwise, there is no procession – there is no room.

THE CEREMONY

The groom or best man hands the certificate of
marriage or licence to the registrar, who then begins the
ceremony by reading from a book much as the minister
or priest in a church does. The wording is simpler and
there is no reference to God, but the sentiments are the
same: that marriage is not to be entered into lightly; that
the couple must know of no cause why they are not free
to marry; and that they pledge themselves to each other.

The vows

The vows are not as poetic as those taken in a church:
for example, there are no promises of 'in sickness and
in health' or 'till death us do part', but they are still as
binding.

Exchanging rings

While taking the vows, the bride and groom may exchange rings. Although these have no significance in a register office wedding, they do form part of the convention of marriage, and many couples may not feel married without them.

AFTER THE CEREMONY

At this point, the couple are legally married and the ceremony is over. It has perhaps taken between 10 and 20 minutes – far shorter than the average church wedding. After the signing of the register by the bridal couple, witnesses, superintendent registrar and registrar, the wedding party is expected to leave promptly to make way for the next couple. The bride and groom may choose to leave the room first, followed by attendants and guests.

Taking photographs

As with a church wedding, the time for photographs is after the ceremony. It should be remembered, however, that, unlike a church, other business is being conducted in the same building, so a lengthy photographic session is likely to be interrupted by people coming and going. It is therefore better to restrict the number of photographs at this stage (in any case, most register office buildings do not make attractive backdrops) in favour of a more relaxed session at the reception venue.

Overleaf is a checklist for getting married in a register office.

Register office checklist

Before the day

- Decide in which register office you wish to be married
- Check with register office that you fulfil the residence requirements
- Make an appointment to see the superintendent registrar
- Take with you your birth certificates, and, if applicable, evidence that a previous marriage is over
- Pay for the marriage notice to be posted
- If two districts are involved, collect the certificate of marriage from the second district when issued, 21 days later
- If marrying by licence, collect and pay for it one day after the notice is posted
- Ask to see the room where the ceremony will be
- Choose the witnesses, minimum two
- Decide who is to come to the ceremony and who is to come to the reception only. Send out invitations accordingly

On the day

- If applicable, take the certificate of marriage from the second district with you to the register office
- Arrive at the register office in good time
- Pay the registrar the fee when you enter the marriage room
- Approach the registrar with your witnesses. The guests may be seated behind on chairs provided
- Sign the register after the ceremony
- Leave the room promptly to make way for the next wedding party
- Keep the photographic session on the register office steps brief

6. Church weddings

Although a church wedding has a religious dimension, in which the couple seek to have their union sanctified in the presence of God, it is, first and foremost, a civil ceremony. It has to be recognized by law and performed by a clergyman who is legally registered to perform the ceremony. In the Roman Catholic and Nonconformist Churches, for instance, a couple must obtain a superintendent registrar's certificate or certificate and licence from a register office before their marriage may proceed. In some cases, a superintendent registrar may need to be present at the ceremony, if the person conducting the wedding is not registered to do so. See 'Marriage and the law', pp. 36–8 and 42.

Before the day

CHOOSING A CHURCH

Broadly speaking, a couple can marry in any church, as long as the clergyman consents to perform the ceremony. For the Church of England, there is a requirement of at least 15 days' residence in the parish, (see pp. 36, 41 and 42), which either the bride or groom must fulfil. However, couples usually opt for the church at which they worship; the parish church local to either the bride's parents' home, if she still lives there, or her own home; or a local church of their own denomination, such as Roman Catholic or Methodist.

Booking ahead

When the bride and groom have made their decision,
they should lose no time in contacting the clergyman
and in arranging an interview. Many churches are
'booked up' well in advance, especially during
summer, and so the couple should expect to look ahead
about six months in order to be sure of the church
being free for their wedding.

THE INTERVIEW WITH THE CLERGYMAN

This interview is for the clergyman to take down the
particulars of the couple and their requirements, and
possibly to meet them for the first time, if they do not
attend the church. These days, many clergymen take a
dim view of their churches being used as attractive
backdrops for the photographs, where there is little or
no religious commitment. In such cases, a clergyman
may refuse to marry the couple, although the local
parish priest or vicar is unlikely to decline, if his is the
designated church for the area in which the bride or
groom lives. Some may insist on the couple attending
the church until the date of the ceremony before they
will consent to officiate.

Proof of marriageability

A church wedding is also a civil ceremony, and it is the
clergyman's responsibility to check the couple's
eligibility before the marriage can legally take place.
He will need to have proof of age (birth certificate)
and, in the case of a second marriage, marital status (a
certified copy of a former spouse's death certificate or
an original divorce document; see pp. 70-2. In England
and Wales, the decree nisi will suffice, as the wedding

is likely to take place after the divorce becomes
absolute, but the law of Scotland requires the decree
absolute to be produced.).

Setting the date and the time

When everything is in order, a mutually convenient
date can be set. Some churches discourage weddings
during Lent, because it is a time of denial and therefore
not appropriate for celebration and festivity. Most
couples choose to marry on a Saturday to fit in with
their own and guests' work commitments, and between
the hours of 10 a.m. and 4 p.m. to allow time for a
reception which coincides with a meal time. They can,
in fact, marry on any day of the week, but not at any
hour of the day. The law specifies marriages have to
take place between 8 a.m. and 6 p.m. (Jewish marriages
are excepted, see p. 38), with open doors.

The type of ceremony

Depending on the wishes and circumstances of the
bride and groom, their church wedding may be quiet
and discreet with minimum adornments, or formal and
festive with all the trimmings. These include organ
music, bells (if the church has them), a choir and floral
decorations. The clergyman will advise what is
available in his church, and what the costs are. These
vary from church to church and are at the discretion of
the clergyman, unlike the fee for the marriage service
which is fixed.

Decorating the church with flowers

The bride and groom should offer to pay for flowers
which those who usually decorate the church will buy
and arrange for them. If the couple chooses to order
and arrange their own flowers, they should check when

it would be convenient for the flowers to be delivered and arranged. Ideally, the morning of the wedding would be most suitable to ensure the flowers are at their freshest, but there may be other weddings that day which will make this impossible. In fact, if his programme for the day is full, the clergyman may rule against couples arranging their own flowers, as this could involve the displaying and dismantling of several sets of flowers during the course of the day.

Choosing the hymns and readings

Many couples leave the choice of music, hymns and readings to the clergyman, but often they have their favourites which have special significance for them. They can discuss these at the first meeting, or leave it until nearer the time. However, the less well-known the tunes, the more notice the organist will need to learn them. For example, a bride may opt for the 'Here comes the bride' music to begin the service and Mendelssohn's Wedding March to be played as she walks with her new husband down the aisle. But several attractive alternatives exist, such as Jeremiah Clarke's Trumpet Voluntary, which the organist may not play very often. Many couples have fixed ideas about the hymns that they would like to be sung at their wedding. The clergyman of their chosen church will be happy to discuss their wishes and advise on suitability and possible choice of tunes. Most church hymn books divide their contents into themes, and there will be plenty of appropriate hymns to choose from for 'love and marriage'.

Number of hymns

In a standard Church of England service, there would

be three hymns, one at the beginning, the second after
the actual marriage, and the third sung by the
congregation as the couple sign the register. If
communion is included, a fourth hymn may be used
after the sacraments have been taken. But there is no
set rule as to how many hymns may be sung. Time,
however, may dictate the number. Alternatively, the
couple may opt for no hymns: they are not compulsory.
Quaker services, for example, have no music at all.

Non-religious music and readings
Most churches these days are very flexible and will
incorporate a non-religious favourite tune or reading in
the order of service. But the clergyman will draw the
line at the very bizarre – the ceremony is a serious
undertaking and its religious significance should not be
diminished by frivolous accompaniments.

Service sheets
When the couple have consulted the clergyman about
their marriage service, they, or whoever is hosting the
wedding, may arrange for service sheets to be printed
and made available to the guests at the church door on
the day. The ushers are usually responsible for their
distribution. A simple order of service might be such as
that shown overleaf.

Music during the signing of the register
Instead of a hymn during the signing of the register, a
selected piece of music may be played. But the couple
should check with the clergyman the musical capacity
of the organist; a hymn tune he or she knows will
sound better than a couple's favourite piece of classical
music (that the organist does not know) played
hesitantly.

Ceremony without a service sheet
The couple may opt to have no service sheet at all.
Most denominations have a set order of service printed
in their prayer or order of services books, and most
hymns appear in the churches' own hymn books.

Service sheet: example

The procession: Trumpet Voluntary (Jeremiah Clarke)

Introduction

Hymn: Love divine, all loves excelling
(the full text should be printed here)

The marriage between
Miss Jacqueline Jackson
and
Mr William Barclay

Hymn: Lead us Heavenly Father, lead us
(again, full text)

The Sermon

The signing of the register

Hymn: The King of love my shepherd is
(full text)

The recession: Wedding March (Felix Mendelssohn)

Payment
Traditionally, the groom pays for the marriage
ceremony and attendant costs, and may either settle the
account in advance or leave it to his best man on the
day, whichever is preferred by the clergyman involved.
These extras should be arranged with the latter as soon
as possible, as he will have a number of people – the
organist, choristers and bellringers – to organize for
that date.

Number of guests
Finally, it is wise to discuss with the clergyman the
number of guests likely to attend, especially if the
church is small. There may be a limit on numbers to
comply with fire regulations, for example. Also, the
couple should find out at this point – and communicate
the answers to the ushers and guests who enquire –
whether the clergyman will allow photographs or
videotaping during the service, or the throwing of
confetti outside the church door. All clergymen have
different views on this, with objections usually based
on disturbance and mess. There is no point ruining the
day and annoying the clergyman.

THE REHEARSAL
Once the date for the wedding has been fixed, the
clergyman may also request that the couple attends a
short weekly course of meetings to discuss the
significance of marriage and the religious implications.
If not, he will certainly insist on a rehearsal of the
ceremony, probably in the week before the wedding.
This is so that the main participants know the
procedure, thereby minimizing the risk of confusion on

the day. The bride, groom, best man and chief
bridesmaid attend this rehearsal. The clergyman takes
them through the order of service, and shows them
where they stand in the church. At this point, it would
be courteous to ask the clergyman if he would like to
come to the reception. Very often, he will decline if he
has another marriage ceremony to perform, or he will
accept, particularly if he knows the family well.

On the day

ARRIVAL OF THE PARTICIPANTS

Traditionally, the groom arrives at the church before
the bride, but he does not have to get there before the
guests, who will have been looked after by the ushers
and seated in their appropriate places well before the
ceremony is due to begin. The bride's mother is not
with her daughter's party, and is the last to take her
place before the bride is escorted up the aisle.

Arrival of the groom

The groom and his best man arrive in sufficient time to
attend to any last-minute arrangements with the
clergyman and to take their places. They sit in the front
pew on the right-hand side of the aisle, facing the altar,
the groom next to the aisle. The groom's family and
friends will be sitting behind them, while the bride's
party sits on the left-hand side. If the couple has
decided to have photographs taken of the groom
entering the church, then he should allow an extra five
minutes for this to be done.

Arrival of the bride

The bride makes her entrance into the church on the

right arm of her father, or the relative or friend who is
'giving her away', and has her face covered with her
veil (if she is wearing one). Behind them, in the
processional (see pp. 98-9), come the chief bridesmaid,
then any other bridesmaids and pageboys. The groom
and best man stand up as soon as the bride enters the
church. If they cannot see her immediately, they will
know she has arrived when the organist starts to play
the bridal march. The groom turns in welcome as his
bride and her party draw level with him, and (if
wearing one) she lifts her veil to reveal her face.

Where the clergyman stands
The minister will be waiting for them, either in front of
the altar rails or on the chancel steps, depending on the
size and layout of the church. He will beckon them to
stand before him. The bride's father and the best man
also approach.

ORDER OF SERVICE
Declaring intent to marry
Depending on the style of service practised by the
clergyman or chosen by the couple, a hymn may be
sung or the minister may begin the service straight
away. He states the reason for the gathering and asks if
there is anyone who knows of any impediment to the
marriage and, if so, he should make it known or
'forever hold his peace'. If there is no objection, the
clergyman asks of the couple in turn, the groom first,
whether it is their intention to marry the other, to which
each replies: 'I will'.

Giving away of the bride
The clergyman then asks who is giving the bride in

The processional (left)

1 Groom
2 Best man
3 Clergyman
4 Bride's father
5 Bride
6 Chief bridesmaid
7 Bride's attendants
8 Bride's mother
9 Groom's parents
10 Bride's brothers, sisters, grandparents
11 Groom's brothers, sisters, grandparents
12 Bride's aunts, uncles
13 Groom's aunts, uncles
14 Parents of attendants
15 Parents of ushers
16 Bride's friends
17 Groom's friends

marriage, to which her father replies, and passes his daughter's right hand to the clergyman who gives it to the groom. The bride's father then steps back from the couple, the responsibility for his daughter now passing to her future husband (see p. 254).

Exchange of vows

At this point, the vows are taken, first by the groom, then the bride. The best man places the ring(s) on the prayer book proffered by the clergyman, and the groom places it on the bride's ring finger. The bride may also do this for the groom. The clergyman pronounces them man and wife, and they are married in the eyes of the church. Even so, they are not married in the eyes of the law until they have signed the marriage register, which is usually located in the vestry to the side of the church.

Holy Communion/Nuptial Mass

In a simple service, the bridal party will proceed to the vestry immediately, but usually the minister will deliver a short sermon and one or two hymns are sung before the signing of the register takes place. If the couple has

The ceremony (left)

1 Clergyman	**5** Best man
2 Bride's father	**6** Chief bridesmaid
3 Bride	**7** Bride's attendants
4 Groom	

chosen to have a Nuptial Mass in the Roman Catholic
ceremony, it will take place at this point, as will the
celebration of Holy Communion in the Protestant
denominations.

Signing the register

The bridal party consists of the bride and groom,
followed by the best man and chief bridesmaid, the
groom's father and the bride's mother, the bride's father
with the groom's mother, with any other bridesmaids
and pages bringing up the rear. The marriage register
and certificate will have been prepared beforehand by
the clergyman with all the relevant details of the
marriage, so all that is necessary is for the bridal couple
to sign the register and certificate, and for the best man
and chief bridesmaid (usually) to sign the documents as
witnesses. At this point, even a clergyman who has
forbidden photographs to be taken of the service will
probably allow the photographer to record the signing
of the register. The clergyman then hands the marriage
certificate to the groom.

Leaving the church

The bridal party emerges from the vestry and recesses
down the aisle to a triumphant, uplifting march. The
bride and groom leave together, followed by the others
in the order shown overleaf. They walk between the
rows of guests until they reach the church door, where

The recessional (left)

1 Groom	**7**	Adult bridesmaid
2 Bride	**8**	Groom's father
3 Best man	**9**	Bride's mother
4 Chief bridesmaid	**10**	Bride's father
5 Child attendants	**11**	Groom's mother
6 Ushers		

the photographer will capture the scene. The guests make their way out of the church in no particular order. The best man may return briefly to settle the charges for the ceremony on the behalf of the groom, if this has not been done already.

AFTER THE CEREMONY

Now is the time that most of the wedding photographs are taken. Most churches have some limited space around the buildings in which a wedding party may pose. The best man organizes the relevant people to be included in the prearranged list of photographs. When this has been done, he signals that it is time to leave for the reception. The newlyweds leave first in the bridal car, with the the couple's parents and bridesmaids and best man in following cars.

Overleaf are a checklist for getting married in a church and a countdown of events at church in the hour before a traditional ceremony.

Church checklist
Before the day

- Decide in which church the wedding will be
- Make an appointment to see the minister
- Take along proof of eligibility
- Discuss with him dates and types of service
- Agree costs and either pay now or arrange to do so after the ceremony
- The groom should see his vicar to coordinate the reading of the banns in both churches, if he comes from a different (Anglican) parish
- Attend any course of pre-wedding meetings requested by the minister
- The bride, groom, best man and chief bridesmaid meet the minister for a rehearsal in the week before the wedding is due to take place.

On the day

- The groom should arrive at the church in advance of the bride, together with the best man who should make sure he has the wedding ring(s)
- The bride arrives with her father and attendants and proceeds up the aisle
- A hymn may be sung at this point or the clergyman may simply begin the service
- The couple exchange vows and rings
- A sermon may be delivered, Holy Communion taken or Nuptial Mass said
- The bridal party proceeds to the vestry to sign the register
- The party recesses down the aisle and out of the church

Countdown at the church

1 hour

- Ushers arrive at the church and seat early guests

20 – 30 minutes

- Minister arrives
- Groom and best man arrive
- Photographs
- Minister and groom check the entry in the register
- Best man pays the minister on the groom's behalf
- Music starts

10 minutes

- Bride's mother arrives
- Bridesmaids arrive
- Photographs
- Everyone positions themselves for processional

5 minutes

- Bride and her father arrive
- Photographs
- Bride, her father and the bridesmaids line up for the processional
- Minister, groom and best man take their places at the altar

7. Arranging the reception

Before the day

CHOOSING THE TYPE OF RECEPTION
The many types of reception from which a bridal
couple may choose fit into two categories: formal and
informal. The former may range from a grand hall with
a five-course, sit-down meal followed by dancing to a
live orchestra, or a small lunch for close relatives and
friends in a good-class hotel, to a marquee in the
garden of the bride's parents' home, using a firm of
caterers. The latter may be in a hotel but with an
informal buffet, in a hired hall with caterers or relatives
providing the food, or in the bride's parents' home with
home cooking. Ultimately, though, the choice will be
dictated by the budget.

Planning in advance
The planning should begin as soon as the wedding date
is set. As a guide, wherever outside firms are involved
– reception rooms, caterers, wine merchants, florists, a
band, for instance – it is best to book at least three
months in advance to make sure of the date. Popular
venues may need to be reserved even earlier, possibly
six months to a year before the wedding date.

CHOOSING THE VENUE
Where the reception is to be held very much depends
on the number of guests envisaged.

Large numbers of guests
A hall
With upwards of 100 guests, the bridal couple should
be thinking in terms of rooms that are designed
specifically for holding receptions. This is because
they are more likely to have sufficient ancillary
facilities, such as parking space, side rooms (for
receiving guests, displaying presents, and for the bridal
couple to change into their going-away outfits),
cloakrooms and lavatories than, say, a church, or other
hired, hall. Some church halls can accommodate up to
100 guests comfortably, and they may have other
facilities such as kitchens and cloakrooms.

A marquee
A large gathering could also be entertained in a large
marquee on the lawn of the bride's parents' home, if it
is big enough. However, parking space *must* be taken
into account (if the neighbours are not to be enraged by
a streetful of cars), along with lavatory and washing
facilities, if the guests are to be accommodated
comfortably. Many firms of caterers will organize
portable facilities to be removed as soon as the
celebrations finish.

Small numbers of guests
Hotels and catering establishments
Smaller gatherings give the bridal couple more venues
to choose from, with a variety of services offered. The
larger hotels or establishments catering for receptions
have a number of rooms to suit most gatherings,
ranging from a small lunch parlour to a grand
ballroom. Many hotels also offer a wedding service.

This may include
- a variety of menus that differ by price per head;
- arrangement of tables according to a seating plan;
- provision of table decorations;
- provision of a Master of Ceremonies, who will help to organize the receiving line, present the bride and groom to the seated guests, introduce the speeches and cutting of the cake, and so on.

At home

If the reception is likely to be more modest, the bride, or her parents, may consider seriously the possibility of having the wedding reception at home. One advantage is the intimate atmosphere which would put the guests at ease, another is the opportunity to cut costs and organize the catering personally.

Arranging the date and time

When a venue has been chosen, the couple or the bride's mother should make an appointment with the person in charge of the rooms to be hired – the manager, in the case of a hotel or reception hall, or the lettings officer for other premises, such as a church hall. They should discuss the date, times and likely numbers, and what is included in the cost.

TYPE OF MEAL

Cost is likely to play a large part in selecting the type of meal offered to guests, but also important is the time the reception is to take place.

Cost and time

A formal meal will take longer than an informal buffet, so time may be a deciding factor. Otherwise, cost and preference will dictate the choice. A formal, three- or four-course meal provided by caterers will be more expensive per head than a buffet, unless the food chosen for the former is very plain or very exotic for the latter. This is because a formal meal entails extra staff to prepare and cook food on the spot, and waiters and waitresses to serve the food and clear the tables. This, however, is usually included in the charge per head and is not an extra cost.

CHOOSING A CATERER

If the chosen reception venue does its own catering and has a good reputation, the bridal couple need not worry about finding caterers. Otherwise, recommendation is the safest way of ensuring quality in the catering service which a couple eventually chooses. All firms will guarantee good service to obtain the business, but the day is really too important to risk staking its success on an unknown quantity.

Preliminary arrangements

All the firms that have been recommended should be contacted, first to find out if they can take the booking for the required date, then to obtain sample menus and a list of charges and services offered. The couple or the bride's parents should then make an appointment to see the manager or whoever will be in charge on the day, to discuss types of food and ask pertinent questions.

Questions to ask the caterers

● Do they cater for special dietary needs, for example, diabetics or vegetarians (very important if the meal is to be a set menu)?

● Do they provide wine-waiter service, whether or not

they provide the wine?

- If they are to provide the wine, do they charge for bottles of wine ordered but not opened?
- How much notice of final numbers do they need?
- Can they organize the cutting of the cake for the guests?
- Do they take care of all the clearing away?
- When is the bill to be settled?
- If the reception is at the bride's parents' home, do they bring the food ready-cooked or do they require use of the kitchen?

This is the time to take care of any special requirements and to iron out any foreseeable difficulties.

CHOOSING THE TYPE OF FOOD

A firm of caterers specializing in wedding receptions will be able to suggest a variety of food combinations to suit most budgets. A buffet meal provides the most scope. There are two sorts of buffet: finger and fork.

Finger buffet

The food is prepared so guests can eat without need for a table or cutlery, enabling them to mingle and eat at the same time. Examples of finger food include: canapés, small sandwiches, individual cakes, chicken drumsticks, and raw vegetables (crudités) with savoury dips. A sample menu is given opposite.

Evening celebrations

A finger buffet is also an excellent way of providing food for guests who are coming to the evening celebrations (those who were not invited to the ceremony or the formal meal). Some hotels offer this option and provide menus that differ according to price.

Sample menu: finger buffet

Assorted sandwiches
Vol-au-vents
Sausage rolls
Raw vegetables: strips of red, green, yellow, orange
peppers; cucumber; carrot; celery; florets of
cauliflower
Savoury dips: cheese; blue cheese; garlic and onion;
yoghurt and cucumber; avocado (guacamole); Indian
spiced (tikka); or Mexican spiced
Cheese straws
Savoury biscuits
Chicken drumsticks in savoury or spicy batter
Cocktail sausages on sticks
Goujons (thin strips of fish fried in batter)
Stuffed eggs
Asparagus rolls

Small cakes, pies, biscuits

Tea and coffee, served with mints or petits fours

Fork buffet

A fork buffet can offer an almost unlimited choice of
food, from cold meats and fish with a variety of salads
to hot dishes which can include chicken pieces,
sausages, even a curry with rice. But it also requires the
use of cutlery and is best chosen if the guests all have
an opportunity to sit down. If they do not, then eating
could be very awkward and, perhaps, distressing. A
sample fork buffet menu is given overleaf.

Sample menu: fork buffet

Starters
Duck or liver paté with toast and garnish
Egg mayonnaise
Raw vegetables and dips
Melon, ready sliced and dressed, with strips of
Parma ham
Avocado, prepared for forks, with dressing

Main courses
A variety of cooked, cold meats: roast pork, beef,
chicken, turkey and game
Fresh or smoked salmon
Portions of quiche: meat and vegetarian
Hot portions of chicken or turkey with a sauce
Curry and rice
Pasta and sauce (not spaghetti – too messy to cut)
Various salads: green; tomato and onion; potato;
potato and onion; celery and apple; sliced
frankfurters and pasta; couscous; winter salad
(white cabbage, carrot and onion, shredded); red and
green peppers; mixed beans

Desserts
Trifle
Fruit sorbet
Fruit pie
Chocolate fudge cake
Lemon meringue
Cheesecake
Fresh fruit
Profiteroles (small choux pastry balls with cream filling) and
chocolate sauce
All served with cream

Cheeseboard

Tea and coffee, served with mints or petits fours

Formal meal

A formal meal is limiting because usually only one choice is offered (apart from special dietary needs), which must appeal to all the guests especially if children are to be present. (A varied menu can be ordered, but obviously, this will be reflected in the cost.) It is safe, therefore, to opt for standard fare – soup or a well-known appetizer to start, meat with vegetables as the main course, followed by fruit (fresh or salad) for dessert. It may not sound exciting, but it is more important to make sure that guests can eat what is offered them than to try to make an impression with originality. If the reception is held in an hotel or restaurant, however, the menu might include two or three dishes for each course from which the guests could choose.

Sample menu: formal meal

Starters
Soup
Melon (alone or with ginger or Parma ham)
Avocado with dressing
Egg mayonnaise
Asparagus with hollandaise sauce
Prawn cocktail
Seafood cocktail (crab, salmon, prawn)
Smoked salmon

Main courses

A *roast meat*: pork; beef; lamb; chicken; turkey; game birds
(pheasant, grouse [in season])
Dressed meats: beef Wellington (fillet in a pastry
crust); pork medallions in a sauce; chicken with ham and
mushroom and cheese sauce (with or without
spices); chicken Kiev (with garlic and herbs encased,
in breadcrumbs)
Fish: fresh salmon; Dover sole; lemon sole; halibut
steak (all with or without a light sauce)
Vegetarian: vegetable lasagne or cutlets; omelette

A *selection of vegetables*: carrots; parsnips; sprouts; cauliflower
(with or without cheese sauce);
broccoli; green beans; petits pois; mangetouts

Side salads: tomato; green or mixed
Potatoes: roast; boiled new (in or out of skins);
croquets; sautéed; Lyonnaise (sliced and baked with
chopped onions in a cheese sauce)

Desserts

Any of the dessert dishes served with the fork buffet
Hot pies: apple; blackberry and apple; apricot
Summer pudding
Chocolate or fruit mousse
Ice-cream confections

Cheeseboard

Tea and coffee, served with mints or petits fours

Sit-down buffet

A choice of combining the formal meal and buffet
exists for those couples who want the ceremony of the
former but without the cost. They can opt for a buffet

meal where the guests serve themselves and then sit at specific places laid out for them on a seating plan. This way, each guest is assured of a seat, while the bridal couple (or the bride's parents) have some control over who sits with whom.

CATERING AT HOME
The same choices hold for couples (or the bride's parents) who decide to have the reception at home, but call in outside caterers. However, if they decide to do their own catering, then their options are limited to what may be prepared in advance.

Planning
Couples must think very carefully before embarking on their own catering for all but the most modest of receptions (up to 30 people). They should not underestimate the time, effort or freezer space that is required to cater for a larger party. It is as well to bear in mind that, on the day, the setting out will have to be done at the same time as the preparations for the ceremony.

Type of meal
However, if they are confident they can cope, then a buffet is the best option, mostly because the food can be prepared in advance. A finger buffet is even better, as quantities of food can be more accurately estimated. Professional caterers allow 15 to 20 items of food per guest, so the couple (or bride's mother) can simply multiply this by the number of guests expected.

China, cutlery and glassware
Food is only one aspect, however. The home caterer should make sure there is sufficient china, cutlery and

glassware for all the guests. Often, relatives will offer
to lend whole sets of each to meet demand; otherwise,
these items may have to be hired. The china and cutlery
can be hired from specialist firms, while the glasses are
sometimes offered – for hire or free – by the off-licence
or wine merchant who is supplying the drinks. (He may
also supply ice.)

CHOOSING WHAT TO DRINK
Before the meal
It is customary for guests to be offered a drink upon
arriving at the reception venue. Often, this is a glass of
sherry, but red or white wine is acceptable. If the
budget allows, champagne may be served as a
welcoming drink, or buck's fizz – champagne and fresh
orange juice – which is more economical but also
provides a refreshing and special alternative to sherry.
One advantage of buck's fizz is that all drinks look the
same, therefore the individual guest may be able to
request smaller amounts of champagne, or none at all,
without seeming to refuse the hospitality. Soft drinks
also should be offered, for non-drinkers, drivers and
children. Most guests will only have the one drink prior
to eating. Calculations for quantity can be based on six
glasses of wine, six glasses of champagne (12 if
serving buck's fizz) and about seven schooners of
sherry from each bottle.
With the meal
Most couples choose wines to complement their chosen
meal, but some offer beer, depending on the known
preferences of some of the guests. A caterer will be
able to offer a wide selection of suitable wines, but

they will be charged at restaurant prices, which are roughly double the retail price. Some caterers will allow wine to be supplied from another source, and just charge for opening and serving ('corkage'). Some will not, however, for business reasons, and so it is worth asking at the outset because it will affect the final cost of the meal.

Choosing wines to suit the menu

Wherever the wine comes from, wine to suit all tastes should be selected, for the same reasons a fairly standard menu is chosen for the main meal. This does not mean selecting a bland variety, however. Most caterers and wine merchants will be happy to advise a good quality selection to complement the chosen menu.

Red or white, sweet or dry?

Broadly speaking, red wine is drunk with red meat, white with white meat, fowl or fish. The white wine served with the main course should be medium to dry, while a sweet variety may be served as a dessert wine. A white wine may also be served as an aperitif, perhaps with the starter. The general rule is that red wine is never served before white, because it overpowers the palate, and a sweet white wine should not be served before a dry variety, for the same reason.

Calculating quantities

When calculating quantities, at least half-a-bottle of wine should be allowed per guest, or three glasses, possibly four if a variety of wines are to be served. However, the number of bottles necessary really depends on whether the guests are heavy wine drinkers. If not, then most may just sip at one glass to be sociable, and therefore much less needs to be ordered.

Non-alcoholic drinks

Non-alcoholic drinks should be available throughout the meal. These need not be confined to the usual fruit juices, but could include alcohol-free wines or even imaginative cocktails which contain no alcohol. The couple should check with the caterer or bar manager at the time of booking. Of course, if the couple (or the bride's parents) are providing the food and drink themselves, there does not need to be a limit to the originality and variety of the soft drinks offered.

Wine for the toasts

Champagne

The bride and groom are traditionally toasted in champagne. Nowadays, most supermarkets and wine merchants offer reasonable quality champagne at affordable prices, so this most luxurious of drinks is well within the reach of many budgets. Of course, it is more expensive if ordered through the caterers.

Sparkling wine

If the budget cannot tolerate champagne, even at just one glass per guest, then a good quality sparkling wine makes an adequate substitute at perhaps half the price. If the bridal couple feels their wedding is not complete without champagne, however, they may order just one or two bottles for the bridal party and serve sparkling wine to the main body of the guests.

Drinks for the evening

Deciding how to provide the drinks

Many couples organize an evening of music and dancing to round off the celebrations, whether a live band or disco. Most reception halls have a bar in the dancing area, from which the guests may obtain drinks.

Who pays for these evening drinks is often a source of
worry at the planning stage of the reception, because it
is the one area over which the hosts have no control
and cannot budget for. Unless the couple (or the bride's
parents) have unlimited funds, or know their guests
well enough to have a fair idea of the amount they
collectively will drink, then they should think carefully
about guaranteeing an open bar for the duration of the
evening.

Ways of paying for the drinks
There are two solutions. One is to arrange with the
caterer, or the reception or hired-hall manager, to put a
limited amount of money 'behind the bar' for guests'
drinks. When this has run out, then the guests must pay
for any more they might want. Alternatively, the best
man may announce, as he invites the guests to continue
the celebrations after the speeches, that a 'cash bar'
will operate during the evening. This means that no
money has been set aside, and guests must pay for all
their drinks thereafter.

Drinks provided by the hosts
This dilemma does not arise, however, where the
reception is held at home or in the local church hall. As
alcohol is not on sale, the hosts will be providing all
the drinks. The couple should bear in mind that
Methodist churches do not allow the consumption of
alcohol on their premises.

WHAT DRINKS SHOULD YOU BUY ?
When planning the reception, list the stages and decide
what sort of drinks are appropriate for each. The table
(overleaf) offers possible ideas.

1 Arrival at reception
Sherry, port, madeira, vermouth, champagne, champagne cocktails, punch, hot punch (for winter), soft drinks for children and drivers.

2 During the meal
Wine (red, white, rosé), soft drinks.

3 Toasts
Champagne, sparkling wine, sparkling fruit juices.

4 After dinner
Provide your own bar (spirits, liqueurs, wine, beer and cider, soft drinks). Bar drinks available.

Handy measures

Small jigger	1 fl oz
Small wine glass	2 fl oz
Cocktail glass	1/4 pint
Sherry glass	1/4 pint
Large wine glass	1/4 pint
Tumbler	1/2 pint

HOW MUCH DRINK SHOULD YOU BUY?

Consider the stages of the celebration, and estimate how much each guest can be expected to drink. The table (opposite) offers a guide for calculating the number of bottles needed. Adjust the figures if guests tend to drink more or less than average, or if they are teetotal or driving home straight after the reception.

	Drink	Allowance per person	Glasses per bottle	Bottles required per 20 guests
Arrival at reception	Sherry	2 glasses	10-12 (²/₃ full)	4
	Champagne or sparkling wine	2 glasses	6-8 (almost full)	6-8
During meal	Wine (red/white/rosé?)	3-4 glasses	6-8 (²/₃ full)	8-10
	Champagne or sparkling wine	3 glasses	6-8 (almost full)	8-10
Toasts	Champagne	1 glass	6-8 (almost full)	3
After dinner	Whisky, Brandy, Gin	3-4 glasses	24 (bar measures)	1-2
	Liqueurs	2-3 glasses	32 (bar measures)	1-2
	Squash (average bottle)	3-4 glasses	18 (medium/long drinks)	4
	Tonic/soda/juices	3-4 glasses	1 (long mixer) or 2 (short ones)	30-80

CHOOSING MUSIC FOR THE EVENING

The choice of music for the evening celebrations
largely depends on the taste of the bride and groom,
and on the size of the reception. A large gathering of
between 200 and 300 guests in a grand ballroom needs
an orchestra or dance band, whereas a smaller event
may be better with a disc jockey playing records.
Again, cost may be the deciding factor.

Who organizes the music

Most caterers can organize music for the evening, but
often a couple have their own preference. They should
check at the time of booking the reception room or
hired hall that they are free to provide their own music,
if that is what they want.

Type of music

Many couples want to round off the day sociably with
music they can dance to, and so opt for 'middle-of-the-
road' sounds. However, if they do expect their guests to
dance, then the music should be lively and not of a
background variety. Conversely, the music should not
be so frenetic or loud that guests who opt not to dance
find it impossible to talk in a normal tone of voice.

THE WEDDING CAKE

The highlight of every wedding reception is the cutting
of the cake by the bride and groom. It symbolizes their
togetherness and allows the guests to share in this
happiness. A wedding cake has to be organized as a
separate item, not just as part of the catering. First,
timing is essential. The couple's plans for their cake
should be drawn up as soon as they have settled on the
type of reception and venue.

Ordering the cake well in advance

A many-tiered cake will take months to make,
particularly if the traditional fruit cake is chosen. The
cake must be made, allowed to mature, then
marzipanned, iced and decorated. It would be wise to
allow about three months for all this to take place
comfortably, in order to ensure complete readiness on
the day. Smaller versions or different cake types – a
sponge, for example – will take less time, but the
couple should not leave this important item until the
last minute. Even a ready-made cake may need to be
ordered a few weeks in advance. The options for
providing a wedding cake are listed below.

Options for providing a wedding cake

- Buying a standard cake from a reputable
  confectioners
- Having a cake made to order by a specialist
- Having a cake made by a relative or friend and iced
  professionally
- Having the whole cake made and decorated by a
  relative or friend

Whatever is chosen, it is no task for an amateur. It
would be false economy for a couple to try to save the
considerable expense by attempting to have it made
cheaply by a well-meaning relative who is not an
expert. The inexperience will show. However, a
relative or friend (or the bride and groom) who does
have experience of making wedding cakes will save
more than half the price charged by a professional firm
by making it themselves.

Making your own cake

Many people want to make their own wedding cake –
not just for economy's sake, but because home made
cake is tastier and you have the pride of achievement as
well! Here are two recipes for fruit cake. One is very
rich and one is slightly lighter, but either will make an
excellent wedding cake.

Rich fruit cake

The instruction outside the brackets is for a 6 in round
or 5 in square tin. The first instruction inside the
brackets is for an 8 in round or 7 in square tin. The
second instruction inside the brackets is for an 11 in
round or 10 in square tin.

Ingredients

170 (340, 680)g plain flour

¼ (½, 2) level tsp mixed
   spice

½ (½, 2) level tsp
   cinnamon

Pinch (large pinch, ½ tsp)
salt

140 (285, 595)g butter

140 (285, 595)g sugar

Small amount grated
   lemon zest

3 (5, 11) size 4 eggs,
   beaten

½ (1, 2) tbsp treacle

1 (2, 3) tbsp brandy

225 (455, 1135)g currants

115 (200, 395)g raisins

115 (200, 395)g sultanas

55 (140, 285)g glacé
   cherries

30 (85, 200)g chopped
   mixed peel

30 (85, 200)g almonds,
   blanched and flaked

Method

Pre-heat oven to temperature of gas mark
2/300°F/150°C. Grease and double line cake tin. Mix
fruit, nuts, and mixed peel in large bowl. Sift flour, salt
and spices in separate bowl. Cream butter, sugar and

lemon zest together until pale and fluffy. Add eggs to
creamed mixture a little at a time, beating well after
each addition. Fold flour gradually into mixture using
metal spoon. Fold brandy and treacle, then fruit and
nuts, into mixture. Put mixture into prepared tin and
bake at Gas mark 2/300°F/150°C for approximately
2½-3 (3½, 7) hours. Cover with greaseproof paper after
1½ -2 hours to prevent top over-browning. Cool in tin
overnight. Turn out, wrap in double thickness of
greaseproof paper, then store in airtight tin.

Lighter fruit cake

This recipe is adaptable for any size and shape of cake
tin, but the quantities given are for a cake tin of 1 pint
capacity. Multiply up the quantities given as required.

Ingredients

115g plain flour	145g currants
½ level tsp mixed spice	55g sultanas
Pinch salt	55g raisins
85g butter	30g glace cherries,
85g soft brown sugar	chopped
1 size 2 egg, beaten	30g chopped mixed peel

Method

Pre-heat oven to a temperature of Gas mark
2/300°F/150°C. Grease and line the cake tin. Mix fruit
and mixed peel together in a bowl. Sift flour, salt and
mixed spice together into separate bowl. Cream butter
and sugar until pale and fluffy, then beat in egg. Fold in
flour using a metal spoon, then fold in fruit and peel.
Place in prepared tin and bake at Gas mark
2/300°F/150°C until a fine skewer inserted into centre
of the cake comes out clean. Cool in tin, then store
wrapped in greaseproof paper in airtight tin.

Delivery of the cake
The finished wedding cake is usually delivered
unassembled, each tier packed in its own separate box,
to the caterers the afternoon before the wedding. Most
caterers offer an assembly service in their costs. On the
morning of the wedding, they will assemble the cake,
mounting each tier on pillars provided, add final
decorations, vase and flowers (if requested) which have
also been provided, so that the cake is prepared ready
for the reception.

Customs and tradition
The tradition of the wedding cake has ancient roots.
The Roman wedding ceremony included the sharing of
a simple cake (made from salt, water and wheat flour);
this became a spiced, fruit cake later in Britain. Cake
also is used in the wedding ceremonies of some Native
American tribes and the people of Fiji Island.

Fertility
The cake tradition may also be connected to the
fertility rituals of many cultures. Sometimes fruits and
grains are displayed as a gesture of bestowing fertility
upon the newly married couple. One custom – similar
to that of throwing confetti – involved showering the
bride with many small cakes after the wedding.
Sometimes the cakes were even broken over the bride's
head, as in Scotland, where oatcakes were used. The
sharing of food symbolizes the new unity shared by the
couple; the breaking of food (or other objects) is
intended to help with the marriage consummation and
childbirth.

Happiness
One custom from Yorkshire involved throwing a plate

holding pieces of the cake out of the window as the
bride entered her father's home after the wedding. If
the plate remained unbroken on landing, the bride was
destined to be unhappy or wretched. If the plate broke
(as it no doubt usually did!) she was sure to be happy.
In other parts of England, a ring was placed in the
wedding cake; the guests would be invited to cut
themselves slices of cake, and the one who found the
ring was said to be ensured happiness for a year.
One custom that is often still practised involves saving
cake to give to unmarried guests as they leave. They
should place these slices of cake under their pillows
and 'dream on them'; this acts as a charm to improve
their chances of marrying in the future. It is even said
that bridesmaids who sleep with a slice of cake under
their pillows will dream of their future husbands. Small
cake boxes with liners can be specially made up and
used for storing these mementoes of the ceremony.

The size of the cake

- Before you order your wedding cake, you must
first consider how big it needs to be. Remember
to take the following factors into account:
- Each guest attending the reception, and friends
who were unable to attend, should receive a
piece of cake.
- Other acquaintances, such as neighbours or
colleagues at work, may like to receive a
reminder of the day.
- You may also want to save some of the cake for
yourself – some couples save the top tier for a
housewarming, their first wedding anniversary,
or the christening of their first child.

Styles

There are many different styles of cake design, from simple round cakes to ones with elaborate tiers and pillars. The original tiered wedding cake is attributed to a London baker on Ludgate Hill; he is said to have copied the shape of the spire of nearby St Bride's Church, which had been designed by Christopher Wren.

Other, more involved designs for wedding cakes are heart shapes, baskets, even good luck signs like clovers and horseshoes.

Colour schemes

Traditionally, wedding cakes have always been iced in white but there is no reason why you should not choose your own individual scheme. You could develop colours which will appear elsewhere during the wedding – the flowers, bridesmaid's dresses, or hair ribbons, for example – or you could personalize the cake with design features such as your initials, names, and/or the wedding date itself.

TABLE DECORATIONS

Decoration by professionals

A professional caterer will also arrange the table decorations for the reception meal. Floral centrepieces are often chosen to brighten up long tables, or small vases of flowers for individual tables. The bride (or her mother) may wish to order the flowers from the florist providing the bouquets and church flowers, to achieve a coordinated effect, and have them delivered to the reception rooms on the morning of the wedding. The caterers will dress the tables according to instructions.

If the reception is being held in a hotel, some establishments include table decorations in the cost of the service.

Decoration by the hosts/bride

If the reception is to be in a hired hall where the bride or her mother is taking charge of the catering, they should check with the lettings officer, with whom they made the booking, that the hall will be open early on the morning so they may set the tables well in advance of the wedding.

Table stationery

The personal touch can be given to a table display with specially printed menus, napkins, coasters and place cards. Special boxes to send portions of wedding cake to absent friends and relatives are also available. Standard stationery with wedding motifs – bells, silver slippers, for example – can be bought from any large stationers. More personalized items can be ordered from many small printers. They will offer a selection of designs which will include the bride's and groom's names and the date of the wedding, usually printed in gold or silver on white, although there are many other colour combinations from which to choose.

Ordering and delivery of items

About three weeks should be allowed between placing the order and delivery of the finished items, which should be made to the reception rooms the day before the wedding. The caterers will include them when setting out the tables the next day. If the bride or her mother is arranging the catering, then the stationery should be delivered to the relevant home address, never to a hired hall, where there may be no one to receive the package, thus risking it going astray.

SEATING PLAN

If the meal is to be a sit-down affair, whether formal or a buffet, then the caterers will need a seating plan in order to place the name cards correctly. This should be drawn up as soon as all the acceptances to the wedding invitations have been received.

Table configurations

A large wedding party will need careful organization, but most caterers will be happy to discuss table configurations to suit the preferences of the bride and groom. They may opt either for a top table with 'arms'

1 A top table with 'arms' at either end

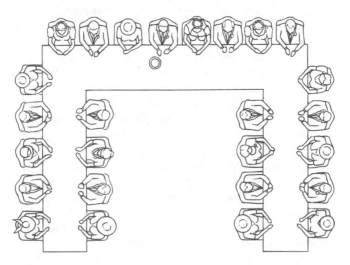

2 A top table with three 'arms', forming a letter E

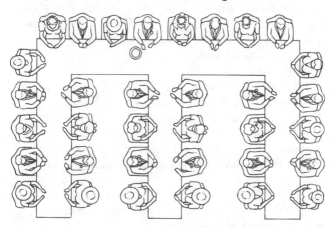

3 A top table with separate tables

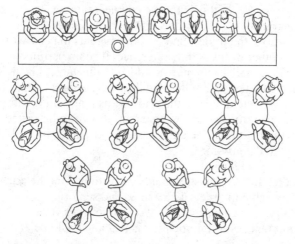

of longer tables which form a letter E, or a top table for
the bridal party with separate tables, seating four, six or
eight people, for the other guests. The advantage of the
latter is that it offers a greater scope for mixing – or
separating – certain guests.

The top table

This usually seats the main bridal party – bride, groom,
their parents, the best man and the bridesmaids.
Traditionally, these are positioned in a specific order.
Looking at the table from the front, some of the
bridesmaids are seated to the left, including the chief
bridesmaid, followed by the groom's father (or the
bride's father), the bride's mother, the groom, the bride,
the bride's father (or the groom's father or the best
man), the groom's mother, the best man, and ending on
the right with other bridesmaids.

Seating members of the bridal party

The purpose of this is for the couple's families to
integrate (see 'The bride's mother', pp. 240-1).
However, the bride's and groom's parents may sit with
each other if this is the preference. If room permits,
brothers and sisters may be added to this table, but at
each end, not within the bridal party. The best man also
may be seated next to the bride – this makes his central
role as toastmaster more apparent. If he is to be seated
next to the bride, the chief bridesmaid will be moved
next to the groom.

Seating the guests

Thereafter, the guests should be positioned on the arms
of the table in order of closeness and seniority –
relatives, friends, and then work colleagues. The
important point to remember is that all should be able

to see the bride and groom. If separate tables are preferred, they can be angled so no one has his or her back fully turned toward the top table.

Using tact and discretion

Tact should be used when seating guests, particularly if there are known family differences. People not on speaking terms in everyday life may not succumb to the charm of the occasion and let bygones be bygones, and an unpleasant atmosphere may result (see pp. 240-1).

Seating children

Small children should be seated with their parents, who can look after their needs (and stop them running about). Older children – over 12 – can be seated with cousins or friends. Although proceedings are not specifically designed to keep the younger members of the party entertained, shrewd seating will ensure enough interest to prevent boredom and, perhaps, disruption.

Entertaining children separately

If the reception is an informal buffet, small children may be tempted to run around and burn off their energy. This can be hazardous if guests are balancing drinks and, perhaps, hot food. Most reception rooms will have smaller side rooms in which children can be entertained. The couple can discuss this with the manager at the first meeting. He may even be able to suggest a children's entertainer, or provide video facilities.

At home

If the bride's family is organizing the reception in a hired hall or at home, then they can organize similar diversions themselves.

Seating/table plan checklist
- Do we want to have a special table for displaying the wedding gifts?
- Do we want to have a special table for displaying the cake so that the photographer and the guests can take photographs?
- Should we place bottles of wine on the tables and, if so, how many bottles should there be per group of people?
- Do we want a side table for storing trays of glasses and champagne for distribution when making the toasts?
- Is the area around the top table free of obstructions so as not to impair any photographs which people may wish to take?
- Can everyone see the bride, groom and any of the other main speakers?
- Are people who want, or need, to be together on the same table?
- Are people who want, or need, to be separated on different tables?
- Have elderly people, who may have special needs, been taken into account?
- Have vegetarians, or other guests who may have special dietary needs, been taken into account?
- Have people who may only want low alcohol, or non-alchoholic, drinks been taken into account?

Seating plans for formal, sit-down reception

Several arrangements for seating at a sit-down reception meal are illustrated on the following pages. The first two are for the most straightforward of parental relationships; these are followed by three arrangements which can accommodate divorced and remarried parents.

In the first, straightforward arrangements, if the top table holding the wedding party is part of a U-shaped design of tables, the additional bridesmaids could be placed along the sides closest to the top table.

If, for some reason, there is tension between the couple's parents, the position of the fathers in the first arrangement can be switched (numbers 2 and 6), so that the bride's parents sit together and the groom's parents sit together, with the bride and groom in between.

Arrangement when the bridal couple's parents are still married

1 Chief bridesmaid
2 Groom's father
3 Bride's mother
4 Groom
5 Bride
6 Bride's father
7 Groom's mother
8 Best man

Alternative arrangement when the bridal couple's parents are still married

1 Groom's mother	**5** Bride
2 Bride's father	**6** Best man
3 Chief bridesmaid	**7** Bride's mother
4 Groom	**8** Groom's father

Arrangement when the bride's parents have divorced and remarried

1 Bride's stepfather	**6** Bride
2 Chief bridesmaid	**7** Bride's father
3 Groom's father	**8** Groom's mother
4 Bride's mother	**9** Best man
5 Groom	**10** Bride's stepmother

Arrangement when the groom's parents have divorced and remarried

1 Best man
2 Groom's stepmother
3 Groom's father
4 Bride's mother
5 Groom
6 Bride
7 Bride's father
8 Groom's mother
9 Groom's stepfather
10 Chief bridesmaid

Arrangement when both sets of parents have divorced and remarried

1 Groom's stepmother
2 Bride's stepfather
3 Chief bridesmaid
4 Groom's father
5 Bride's mother
6 Groom
7 Bride
8 Bride's father
9 Groom's mother
10 Best man
11 Bride's stepmother
12 Groom's stepfather

INSURANCE

It is worth the bride or her parents insuring any personal property which may be left on the reception premises overnight. These include china, cutlery, glassware, possibly cases of wines and spirits, and the cake. Also under the protection of the policy might be the wedding presents, set out for display to the guests on the day. The family insurance broker or any reputable firm will be able to quote terms and offer cover against fire, theft and accidental damage, although the premium for breakables – cups and glasses, for example – might be too high to justify the expense of cover.

Reception checklist
Before the day

- Decide on the type of reception that is wanted
- Choose the venue and check the services offered; book the marquee if needed for a reception at home
- Choose the caterer and discuss menus and wines; advise him of likely numbers
- For a home reception, decide on what to prepare in advance and what to cook on the day; arrange hire of tables, china, cutlery and glassware if needed
- Arrange provision of music if the celebrations are to continue into the evening
- Arrange the making of the wedding cake, printing of table stationery, provision of floral table decorations
- Draw up seating plan, if needed
- Arrange for delivery of all items needed at the reception venue the day before the wedding
- Take out insurance, if needed

On the day

FINAL CHECKS AND PREPARATIONS

If the reception is being held in a hall with outside
caterers, then the managers of both should be contacted,
early on the wedding morning, with the final numbers

On the day check list
For reception rooms

- Advise caterers of final numbers and ensure all
  items have been delivered, including the seating plan
- Arrive at the reception in advance of the guests to
  welcome them
- Make sure they are offered a drink on arrival
- Ensure the best man advises them of bar
  arrangements when he invites them to stay for
  evening celebrations
- Make sure all presents, the couple's wedding outfits
  and the remainder of the cake are taken after the
  celebrations have finished

For a reception at home or a hired hall
with home catering

- Defrost all prepared food and set it out on tables
  (take it to the hired hall as early as possible and
  set it out)
- Make sure all items and hired ware has been
  delivered
- Make sure all guests are able to find a parking space
  near the home or hall
- Clear up the hired hall before the hire time expires

of guests, and to ensure all deliveries have been made
and that there are no last-minute hitches. Items to check
are: the cake, flowers, wines (if a company other than
the caterers is providing them), table decorations and
stationery, and the seating plan.

Food and table arrangements
If the bride or her mother is arranging the food, frozen
items of food should be defrosted as soon as possible;
all the food should be laid out in the hired hall; and
tables should be arranged, if the reception is at home.

Receiving line
Receiving lines are usually designed as a way to
greet guests at the reception following the wedding
ceremony. If some guests, however, have not been
invited to the reception, having a small receiving line
outside the church or other wedding location allows
for goodbyes and good wishes to be exchanged with
the wedding party.

**The order of
people in the
receiving line
at a formal
reception**
1 Bride's mother
2 Bride's father
3 Groom's mother
4 Groom's father
5 Bride
6 Groom

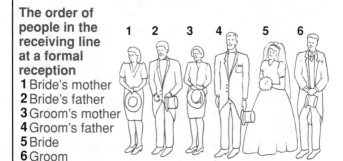

BEFORE THE MEAL
The receiving line

After the ceremony, the immediate bridal party should
arrive at the reception venue ahead of the other guests
in good time to form a welcome line. Tradition dictates
the order of the line. The first to greet the guests are the
bride's mother and father (who are probably the hosts)
followed by the groom's mother and father, and ending
with the bride and groom. If this is likely to take up too
much time – if there are many guests, for example –
then just the bride and groom can receive their guests.

When attendants – such as best man and
bridesmaids – are part of the wedding party, they
should come after the bride and groom in the formal
receiving line, with the best man first, followed by
the chief bridesmaid.

When more complicated parental relationships are
involved (divorced and remarried, for example), it is
often best to have the receiving 'line' made up of
only the bride and groom.

**Alternative order
of people in the
receiving line
(sometimes used
for a less formal
reception)**
1 Bride's mother
2 Groom's mother
3 Bride
4 Groom

Drinks before the meal

After this, the guests should be offered a drink – sherry or wine – before they enter or are seated in the reception room itself. At some Scottish weddings, drinks are served as soon as the guests arrive at the reception (while the wedding party perhaps has more photographs taken). Guests are then presented to the receiving line before being seated for the meal.

AFTER THE MEAL

Toasts and speeches

When the guests have finished eating, the toasts are drunk, after which the best man initiates the speeches. The purposes of the speeches are twofold; firstly, to congratulate the newly married couple and to wish them well for the future and, secondly, to say thank you to certain people. The usual reaction of people who are asked to make a speech at a wedding is extreme nervousness, if not downright panic. Yet, as long as you stick to a few basic guidelines, and familiarize yourself with what you intend to say, making the speech should be relatively painless, if not actually enjoyable.

Numerous publications with ideas on how to compose your thoughts are available. If all else fails, there are also agencies specializing in writing speeches, or in providing a selection of jokes, anecdotes or quotations.

Cutting the cake

After the meal, the best man will organize the cutting of the cake. The caterers – or the bride's mother – will have placed it on the top table (or side table nearby so the guests' view of the bride and groom is not

obstructed) prior to the arrival of the guests.
Traditionally, the bridal couple make the first cut with a
fancy knife. However, it is wise for the cut to have
been started by the caterers or the bride's mother –
particularly if the icing is the hard kind – so the couple
do not have to struggle to make an impression on the
cake. After the cutting, the cake is taken away and the
bottom layer is cut into sufficient portions for every
guest to be offered a piece. Extra pieces may be cut for
absent relatives or friends and sent to them in special,
decorated boxes.

Dancing and the bridal couple's departure
If there is dancing, the bride and groom traditionally
lead the floor, and the more informal festivities get
under way. Depending on flights and hotel bookings,
the bridal couple may leave the reception at an
appointed time. If there are no restrictions, they may
stay later, if the party is going with a swing. Guests
normally feel impolite if they leave before the bride
and groom, so the couple should not leave it too late to
make their departure. Guests may take the opportunity
to throw confetti at this point if it was denied them at
the church.

Clearing up
Gradually, the celebrations come to a close, usually at
an appointed time so that the caterers can clear up. The
best man or other appointed person should make sure
that any presents displayed at the venue, the couple's
bridal clothes and the rest of the wedding cake are
taken away. If the bride's mother has organized the
reception in a hired hall, this must also be cleared
before the period of hire expires.

8. Wedding invitations

Once the couple has decided on, first, the wedding venue (church or register office) and, second, the type of reception (a formal, 'sit-down' meal or a buffet, whether in a hall or at the bride's home), then the task of compiling the guest list and sending out the invitations should be undertaken without delay.

WHEN TO SEND THE INVITATIONS

Depending on how early arrangements for the ceremony and reception have been made, invitations should be sent about two months in advance of the wedding, more if it is to take place in the summer or other popular holiday period, such as Christmas or Easter. Many people make plans for holidays months ahead, and it would be very disappointing – for the guests and the bridal couple – if especially close relatives or friends had to refuse owing to prior arrangements that cannot be cancelled.

COMPILING THE GUEST LIST

Although the invitations are traditionally sent out by the bride's mother, it should not follow that the greater number of guests are from the bride's side of the family. The bride and groom should have an equal opportunity to invite a similar number of guests each.

Equal numbers of guests

Very often, one side of the family is considerably larger than the other, or one of the couple's family and friends come from a different town and many would find difficulty in travelling. Therefore an even split may not be as fair as it sounds. It would not augur well for good relations between the families on the day if, say, many of the bride's close friends have had to be excluded while the groom has had to canvass slight acquaintances to make up the numbers.

Consulting the parents
The bride and groom themselves could iron out any future difficulty by first making a list of all the people they would like to see at their wedding. They should perhaps involve their parents at this early stage, mainly out of courtesy (particularly if it is likely that both sets of parents will be footing the bill) but also to check whether anyone has been forgotten.

Making sure of the numbers
If the number of guests on the list coincides with the number of guests envisaged at the wedding and reception (or the number of guests that can be afforded), then there is no further problem; but if not, then all concerned should decide very quickly who are the essential guests and who may be left out.

Reception only
One way round this dilemma is to invite those who cannot be fitted in at the ceremony (if it is at a small register office, for example) to the reception only (see 'Register office weddings', pp. 82-3). This is a common practice and rarely causes offence to guests, unless, of course, they are close relatives who have been displaced by mere friends!

Cost as the deciding factor
If the major factor in the limitation of numbers is likely to be cost, and as the largest single outlay is the reception, then the solution of inviting guests to the

reception only will not apply. Therefore, a strictly
limited guest list for the wedding and the celebrations
afterwards may be the only answer.

Evening reception only

If the couple would like to involve friends and relatives
who could not be invited to the meal, a dance in the
evening might be the answer. The wording of an
invitation for the celebrations would be much as that
shown in the example on p. 83.

WHO TO INVITE
Family
Weddings tend to be family occasions, and so relatives
in the bride and groom's immediate families and
perhaps one step removed – grandparents, aunts,
uncles, cousins – are always included. Then come close
friends of each of the couple, and possibly work
colleagues, if the bride or groom has known them some
time. Sometimes, too, the bride's mother has a
particularly good neighbour who has helped her during
the time she was bringing up her daughter, and she
would like to include her and/or her family in the
celebrations. (It is unusual for the groom's mother to
express such a preference, although the groom himself
has every right to make the suggestion.)
Friends
However, if the bridal couple are getting married in a
town far away from both their families, then it might be
unrealistic for them to expect large numbers of relatives
to make what may be a difficult and expensive journey.
In this case, most of the invitations will go to friends
the couple have made since moving from home. And in

some cases, neither the bride nor the groom particularly wants a huge wedding in front of relatives they perhaps never see except at just such an occasion. So they may wish to opt for a small gathering of close friends.

WHO SENDS THE INVITATIONS?

Invitations are sent out from the bride's side of the family as, traditionally, they are the hosts and will be meeting the cost. Even if the bill is to be shared, it is still the bride's mother who actually writes, posts and receives replies to the invitations. Some couples prefer to invite their guests more informally, but this should always be done in writing. A casual telephone call does not really fit in with the seriousness of the occasion. However, the couple may want to send the invitations out in their own names. This is acceptable, particularly if they are making some contribution to the cost of the event.

WHAT KIND OF INVITATION?

Shop-bought invitations

Standard, printed invitations with an appropriate design can be obtained from most newsagents, where space is left for the hosts' and guests' names, the name of the bride and groom, the venue (ceremony and reception) and the date and time.

Handwritten invitations

If the wedding is small, perhaps fewer than 20 people, then a decorative, handwritten invitation would give an unusual, personal touch. A greater number would involve quite a bit of time and hard work, and therefore ready-printed invitations would be more suitable.

Custom-printed invitations

For a more personalized version, a small printer would
be able to provide a complete invitation with all this
information (except the name of the guest, of course)
incorporated into the printing, which may be offered in
a choice of typefaces and colours. Many printers who
specialize in this work will also offer a wide range of
designs, from a simple card with a border to a more
fancy design, as a booklet, with embossed print and
even a ribbon.

Cost

Naturally, the cost will vary considerably depending on
the design chosen, and it is wise to set a budget
beforehand.

Schedule

If a small printer is engaged to produce the invitations,
he will need instructions at least two weeks before the
date the invitations are to be sent out.

WORDING THE INVITATION

A wedding is a formal occasion, and therefore the
invitations should reflect this. By tradition, they are
written in the third person rather than the more familiar
'we' and 'you'. The hosts ask the guests for the
pleasure of their company. The invitations also give the
relevant information: who is marrying whom, where
and when. Finally, an invitation asks for a reply, usually
by adding the abbreviation RSVP, which stands for
répondez s'il vous plaît – French for 'Reply, if you
please', and gives an address to which the reply should
be sent. Acceptable wording would be something like
the example given on the facing page.

Wording the invitation: example

Mr and Mrs John Jackson
request the pleasure of the company of
**Mr and Mrs Robin Fisher
and Simon**
at the wedding of their daughter
Jacqueline
to
Mr William Barclay
at St Stephen's Parish Church,
Belle Vale Road, Liverpool
on
Saturday, 22 April 1993 at 2 p.m.
and afterwards at
Woolton Hall, High Street, Woolton.

RSVP
by 24 March 1993

99 Churchfield Road
Liverpool 25
Tel: 051-428 4675

Making replying easy

Although replies should be written to continue the
formality, it may be wise to include a telephone
number, in case there is any query, or so the guests can
indicate acceptance a few days before you receive the
formal reply. A reply card could be enclosed with the
invitation (see p. 155 for an example). It is considered a
courtesy to send this out already stamped.

Alternative forms of address

The guests

The guests should always be addressed individually by

name, both out of courtesy and to indicate exact
numbers. 'The Fisher Family' is too unspecific, as is
'Mr and Mrs Robin Fisher and Family'.

The bride and groom

If the bride and groom are sending out the invitations
themselves, then their names should be substituted for
those of the bride's parents, and the wording from 'at
the wedding of' to the groom's name should be
replaced with 'our wedding'.

Double weddings

Where two sisters are to be married at the same
ceremony, then the names of the elder daughter and her
future husband should appear first on the invitation. If,
say, the wedding is for a daughter and a niece, then the
daughter's name, and her groom's, take precedence.

The bride's parents

The names of the bride's parents alter in format,
depending on status.

Standard forms of address according to status

- Either parent widowed: Mr John Jackson;
  Mrs Ena Jackson
- Parents divorced and in contact: Mr John Jackson
  and Mrs Ena Jackson
- Parents divorced, no longer in contact:
  Mrs Ena Jackson*
- Parents divorced, mother remarried: Mr John
  Jackson and Mrs Ena Roberts
- Parents divorced, no longer in contact, mother
  remarried: Mr and Mrs Philip Roberts*

* If the bride is with her father, then his name, and (if
applicable) the name of his new wife, should be used.

Hosts other than the bride's parent

When the host(s) is not a parent of the bride, then his or her name (or their names) appear at the top of the invitation, and the reference to the relationship with the bride appears instead of 'daughter'. A list of other possible hosts is given below.

Hosts	Bride's relationship
grandparents	granddaughter
aunt and uncle	niece
godparents	goddaughter
foster parents	foster daughter
brother and wife	sister

INCLUDING FURTHER INFORMATION

When you are sending out the wedding invitations it is often helpful for the intended guests if you include a fairly detailed map of the area. Ideally, this should show the route from any major roads to the church or register office, then to the place where the reception is to take place. Variations in the route may cause confusion for guests not familiar with the area, so it is probably better if you decide on the best roads to take. You could also include any information you may have on appropriate hotels, guest houses, or other places offering suitable accommodation for those people who intend staying overnight after the reception is over.

Gift lists

It is not a good idea to include a wedding 'gift list' at this stage as it presumes acceptance of the invitation and, moreover, the offer of a gift. The list should only be sent after the acceptance has been received, and if it has specifically been requested.

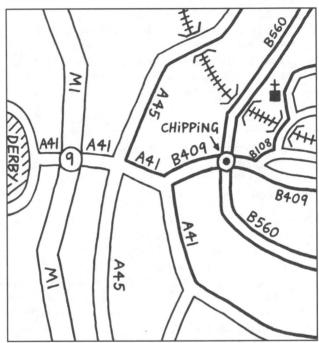

Tina and Bob's wedding is being held at Chipping
Parish Church on Saturday 15th June at 12.00 noon. To
get there, leave the M1 at junction 9, and take the A41
to the junction of the B409 (you will see a pub called
the Fox and Hounds on the left hand corner). The B409
takes you into Chipping. Once there, turn left into the
B108, and then left into the High Street. Cross over the
railway bridge and then turn left into Old Mill Lane.
The church is about 300 yards down on the left.
Parking is available 30 yards further on the right.

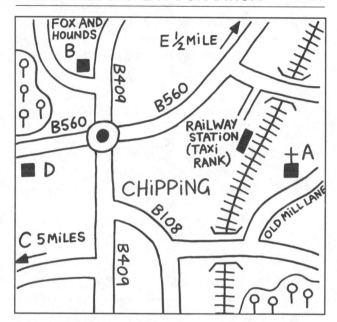

A Chipping Parish Church
(arrive 11.30am for 12.00 start).

B Fox and Hounds
(for reception – sit down at 2.30pm).

C Chilton Hotel
Single £35 per night/Double £50 per night
Tel 0626 321 7654

D Dog and Duck Inn
Single £25 per night/Double £40 per night
Tel 0627 123 4567

E Bell Inn
Single £15 per night/Double £30 per night
Tel 0627 567 1234

Options for your own wedding invitation

---

1   Mr & Mrs Harold Smith request
           the pleasure of the company of

_____

           at the marriage of their daughter
2   <u>Theresa Sarah</u> to <u>John Green</u>
                          at
           St Mary's Church, Bath
     On Saturday 8th November 1993,
3   at 3.00pm
     and afterwards at the Rose and Crown
              for a reception
                   RSVP

4   Address
     100 High Street, Bath, Avon BA12 8TH

---

1 Typeset and printed
2 Typed
3 Calligraphy
4 Word-processed

RECEIVING THE REPLIES

Guests usually respond fairly quickly to a wedding
invitation because they know the bride's mother or the
couple themselves are keen to finalize numbers. So replies
should start to come in within a week of the invitations
being sent out. A list of guests who have been invited
should be drawn up, and the names should be ticked (or
crossed) off as their replies come in. Anybody notoriously
slack in responding should be given a telephone reminder

after two weeks, so the final numbers can be passed to the minister or registrar and, if relevant, the caterers as early as possible.

Reply card: example

> . . . .
> are pleased to accept
> your kind invitation for
> Saturday, 22 April 1993.
>
> Number of guests . . . .

POSTPONEMENT AND CANCELLATION

There may be occasions where a wedding has to be postponed or cancelled – a sudden accident, severe illness or bereavement, for example – and a second notice has to be sent out. Obviously, there is no control over the timing of these events – one may occur on the eve of the wedding – but the couple should try to inform guests of the change in arrangements as soon as possible.

Postponement

If time will not allow a written notification, then all the guests must be telephoned without delay. Otherwise, a notice should be sent out.

Examples of postponement and cancellation notices are given overleaf.

Postponement notice

> Owing to the recent illness of Mrs Jackson's
> mother, the wedding of her daughter
> Jacqueline to Mr William Barclay,
> at St Stephen's church at 2 p.m. on Saturday,
> 22 April 1993, has been postponed until
> 11.30 a.m. on Saturday, 3 July 1993.

Cancellation notice

> Owing to the sudden death of Mr Jackson,
> the wedding of his daughter,
> Jacqueline to Mr William Barclay,
> at St Stephen's Church at 2 p.m. on Saturday,
> 22 April 1993, will not now take place.
> The marriage will be held privately
> at a date to be arranged.

These simple statements of fact are sufficient.
Postponement does not require the return of wedding
presents. With cancellation owing to unfortunate
circumstances in the family and the holding of a private
ceremony, presents may be returned, but the decision
must rest with the couple or the hosts and their
understanding of their guests' wishes. With complete
cancellation, however, presents should definitely be
returned.

Invitation checklist

- Compile your guest list to fit the numbers for the church or register office, and reception
- Check with each set of parents in case of any omissions
- Decide whether some guests are to be invited to the reception only
- Send the invitations in good time for guests to keep the day free
- Decide on the sort of invitation you want: handwritten, standard stationers' or custom-printed
- If the latter, decide on the wording, colours and delivery date with the printer in good time
- Observe custom with titles, e.g. of divorced parents
- Include the following information: names of the hosts; name of the bride and groom; date, time and place of the ceremony; date, time and place of the reception; RSVP; address and telephone number for replies; reply paid card (if preferred)
- Enclose a map if guests are unfamiliar with the district
- Make a list of guests invited and tick (or cross) them off as you receive the replies

WEDDING GIFTS

Once the invitations are organized, preparations should be made for receiving the wedding gifts. Often upon receiving an invitation to a wedding, the invitees (even if they cannot actually attend the ceremony) will want to arrange for the immediate purchase of a gift. It helps if the couple have some idea of the gifts they specifically want or need.

Most guests will assume that the newly wed couple will be setting up house together for the first time and thus will want to give practical household items. If these are not needed (because, for example, the couple are already set up in a home), it is best to advise people beforehand: no one benefits if the gift is either unwanted or unneeded!

Registering

One way to let guests know what items are needed (and to ensure that duplicate items are not given) is to register with a major department store or specialist shop. The couple selects the items they want or need that are available in the shop (making sure the list represents a wide price range to suit different pockets), and the shop holds the list.

A simple word-of-mouth mention, or – although some consider this to be in bad taste – an announcement included with the invitations, can let the invitees know of the list's existence. Guests who wish to use their imagination and creativity to select an unexpected gift can always do so, but those who don't will have an easy option to follow.

The shop then keeps account of which items on the list have already been purchased, so that no duplicate items

are bought. This method is a tremendous help for some
guests, and for the wedding couple.

The gift list

Another option is for the couple to prepare a list of
items they need and either distribute it with the
invitations – again, considered by some to be in bad
taste, but not at all by others – or keep it as a checklist
for any occasions when guests might enquire about
what to give. This has the advantage of allowing the
couple to include virtually any item they want or need,
but also the disadvantage of not preventing the
duplication of purchases.

When drawing up the list, be sure to include a range of
prices and to be specific about what make, model, and
even colour of item is desired. This way, there will be
fewer disappointments when the gifts are received. Try
to list many more items than guests so that no one is
left with only a few choices at the end. If drawing up
your own list, include space to write in who gave what
once the gifts start arriving; the number of gifts can be
daunting and chaos can soon result, especially in the
case of a large wedding.

See the lists on the following pages for examples of
items you might want to include. Furniture and large
appliances are listed, although in most cases these are
too costly for anyone other than close friends or
relatives to give to the wedding couple.

Alternative gifts

Other gifts you may receive are money, travel tickets
and insurance policies. These may be the most useful
types of present for a couple who have already set up
house, or have established professions and lifestyles.

If receiving such gifts, treat them in the same way you would treat traditional gifts: keep track of who gave what and acknowledge all gifts after the wedding, making sure that with cash gifts you indicate to the giver how you plan to use the money.

Kitchen

ITEM	NUMBER	MAKE/MODEL	COLOUR	GIVEN BY

Appliances

ITEM	NUMBER	MAKE/MODEL	COLOUR	GIVEN BY
Blender				
Coffee bean grinder				
Coffee maker				
Dishwasher				
Espresso/cappucino maker				
Food processor				
Ice cream maker				
Microwave oven				
Pressure cooker				
Tea kettle				
Toaster				

Kitchen tools

ITEM	NUMBER	MAKE/MODEL	COLOUR	GIVEN BY
Breadboard				
Breadbin				
Carving board				
Carving knife and fork				
Casserole dish				

Kitchen tools continued

ITEM	NUMBER	MAKE/MODEL	COLOUR	GIVEN BY
Colander				
Corkscrew				
Chopping knives				
Dish drainer				
Fish poacher				
Frying pan				
Garlic press				
Knife sharpener				
Measuring spoons				
Mixing bowls				
Pepper mill				
Place mats				
Salad bowl				
Salt and pepper shakers				
Saucepan				
Scales				
Spice jars				
Spice rack				
Tablecloth				
Tea towels				
Wine cooler				
Wine rack				
Wooden spoons				

China/crockery/cutlery

Bread basket

Kitchen tools continued

ITEM	NUMBER	MAKE/MODEL	COLOUR	GIVEN BY
Butter dish				
Butter knives				
Cereal bowls				
Champagne glasses				
Cheese platter				
Cream jug				
Cups and saucers				
Dessert plates				
Dinner plates				
Drinking glasses				
Egg cups				
Fish-serving knife and fork				
Forks				
Gravy boat				
Jam pot				
Knives				
Liqueur glasses				
Mugs				
Serving dishes				
Serving spoons				
Side plates				
Soup bowls				
Soup spoons				
Spoons				
Sugar bowl				
Water jug				

Kitchen tools continued

ITEM	NUMBER	MAKE/MODEL	COLOUR	GIVEN BY

Wine decanter				
Wine glasses				

Bedroom

ITEM	NUMBER	MAKE/MODEL	COLOUR	GIVEN BY

Furniture

Bedside lamp				
Bedside tables				
Blanket box/tea chest				
Mirror				
Vanity table				
Wardrobe				

Linen

Bedspread				
Blanket				
Duvet (single)				
Duvet (double)				
Duvet cover				
Pillows				
Pillowcases				
Sheets				

Bathroom

ITEM	NUMBER	MAKE/MODEL	COLOUR	GIVEN BY
Bath mat				
Mirror				
Linen bin/basket				
Scales				
Towels				
Wastebin				

Cleaning

ITEM	NUMBER	MAKE/MODEL	COLOUR	GIVEN BY
Carpet sweeper				
Clothes dryer				
Iron				
Ironing board				
Spin dryer				
Vacuum cleaner				
Washing machine				

ITEM	NUMBER	MAKE/MODEL	COLOUR	GIVEN BY

Furniture

Bookcase				
Chairs				
Coffee table				
Dining table				
Sofa				

Appliances

CD rack				
CD player				
Stereo/hi-fi				
Television				
Video cassette recorder				

MISCELLANEOUS

Clock				
Cushions				
Fireplace tools				
Lamp				
Photograph album				
Pictures/Prints				
Plants				
Rug				
Vase				

9. Ordering the flowers

TYPES OF FLOWER ARRANGEMENT
Most brides plan their flowers around the type of
wedding they are having and the colour scheme they
have chosen.
Formal
A grand affair, perhaps in a large church and afterwards
in a reception hall or marquee with hundreds of guests,
requires floral arrangements in proportion to the
occasion. This means fairly stylized displays, both at
the church and at the reception.
Informal
A more informal occasion – a register office wedding
with a small reception at home, for example – can be
adequately catered for with simple vase arrangements
and bunches of flowers. Choosing flowers out of
keeping with the scale of the occasion will lead to an
unsatisfactory effect on the day.

ARRANGING THE FLOWERS
When the bride, or her mother, has decided on the kind
of flowers she wants for the wedding, she needs to
decide whether to employ a professional florist or to
tackle the arrangements herself.
Professional arranging
Unless the style she has chosen is informal, or she is
adept at flower arranging, the bride would be wise to
leave intricate work to a florist. Most of the work will
have to be done immediately before the wedding, at a
time when things are at their most hectic.

Home arranging

There can be a great deal of satisfaction for a bride in creating her own designs; so if she opts to do the flowers herself, she should plan to order them in advance, at about the same time she would if leaving everything to the florist.

FLOWERS FOR THE CHURCH

Checking with the clergyman

Flower arrangements for the church should be discussed with the clergyman at the couple's first appointment with him. They should ask permission to bring in their own displays – this is by no means a foregone conclusion, as there may be circumstances which dictate that outside flowers are not allowed. One of these would be in a church where several weddings are to take place on the same day. It would not be practicable for four or five sets of floral displays to be arranged and dismantled.

Leaving it to the church flower arrangers

The clergyman will advise about floral arrangements, and may suggest that the church decoration is left to those who arrange the flowers for him every week, the couple perhaps making a contribution to the cost so that the flower arrangers may buy in more flowers to make the church more decorative.

The bride or hosts as flower arrangers

This could severely limit a bride who has set her heart on a particular colour scheme to match her bouquet and the bridesmaids' posies. There is no way around it, though, unless she opts to set her wedding date at a time of year which is not so popular and she has more chance of hers being the only wedding on that day. In this case, the clergyman would usually be willing for her relatives or friends, or a florist, to come in either the day before or on the morning of the wedding to decorate the church with her own flowers. The people usually in charge of flower arranging would also probably come in to help her if this is arranged beforehand. The advantage of this is that they are more conversant with the layout of the church and know where to display flowers so they are at their most eye-catching.

What sort of flowers?

Any flowers will look beautiful in a church setting, whether blooms in hot colours to match the blaze of summer, or in cool, tranquil pastels to reflect the solemnity of the occasion. Usually, the chosen flowers are arranged in free-standing displays behind the altar rails (the church will have stands to hold them), in smaller arrangements on the window sills and on the pulpit, and possibly in garlands on the pew-ends. This is an American custom which has become popular in Britain in recent years.

FLOWERS FOR THE REGISTER OFFICE

Many register offices soften a severe decor with fresh flowers which are changed every day. Unlike a church, where weddings are usually conducted on Saturdays, ceremonies can take place in a register office whenever it is open. It is therefore not necessary to make special arrangements for floral decorations, although the office will be open to requests for a special adornment for a particular wedding.

FLOWERS AT THE RECEPTION

The bride has greater scope here for invention, and the setting of the reception will largely dictate the sort of flowers and the scale of arrangements she chooses. Professional reception establishments or hotels, however, may decorate their rooms with flowers to suit the decor as a matter of course. This may form part of the service offered, and should be checked when booking the room. They will usually consent to the bride's own flowers being brought in, but would probably insist they arrive at a particular time to fit in with their own preparations.

Displaying the flowers effectively

The scale of the arrangements depends on the size of the room and the availability of space. One good-size display at the entrance, then smaller arrangements on the tables, will be sufficient to create a pleasing effect. The advantage of table decorations is that they are directly in the view of the guests which maximizes their effect, and that they are movable and so can be positioned elsewhere when the tables are cleared, perhaps in preparation for the evening celebrations.

Flowers for the cake

Many couples feel that flowers add a fresh, finishing touch to the cake, rather than an artificial version or even a plaster bridal couple. A professional caterer can usually supply a small spray of flowers and even a small silver vase in which to display them. They will add the flowers when they assemble the cake on the morning of the wedding. Alternatively, the bride can have her special choice delivered from the florist to tie in with the caterer's plans for the cake.

Practical choice of flowers

The bride should be careful not to choose flowers
which readily droop in the heat; this would spoil the
overall effect and make the cake look unappetizing.

FLOWERS FOR THE WEDDING PARTY
The bride's bouquet

This is the most special flower arrangement of the day
and needs the most care and thought when choosing
style, colour and variety of flower. The bride need not
have a bouquet at all – in fact, tradition dictates she
does not if she opts to wear a hat rather than a veil.
However, most brides would feel their ensemble was
incomplete without a bouquet.

Popular/formal styles and shapes

There are several styles and shapes of bouquet to
choose from. A good florist will be able to show the
bride a brochure depicting a number of examples
which they can copy in her choice of flowers
(assuming they suit the design). The most popular
include the round bouquet of tightly arranged flowers
and the looser 'tear' or 'fall' – where the design is full
at the top and tapers towards the bottom.

Unusual/informal styles and shapes

The bride may choose to have a more informal bouquet
– a simple bunch or even a single bloom, for example –
if her wedding is small and quiet, perhaps a second
wedding, or even a small register office occasion. She
could also opt for a less formal design if she is not
wearing the traditional long, white dress.

Colour scheme

The bride might have set her sights on a particular

colour scheme for her bouquet and will base the colour of the other flower arrangements, and even the colour of the bridesmaids' dresses, on this scheme.

Conversely, she may have decided on the colour for the bridesmaids' dresses and want her flowers to echo the scheme.

Advice from the florist

The florist should be informed of the plan so he or she can advise which flowers are most suitable for providing the correct combination of colour. In a highly colourful scheme, foliage may be chosen to offset the mass of colour. An all-white scheme is often not advisable (not all whites are the same colour): beautiful white lilies, for example, could look yellow and drab set against a dress which is more blue-white.

Bridesmaids' posies

The bridesmaids traditionally carry smaller floral arrangements which complement their dresses. Small girls often look enchanting holding country-style flowers which look as if they have been gathered from the hedgerow.

Headdresses

For her headdress, the bride may choose fresh blooms as opposed to fabric flowers to match her bouquet. Florists are used to making up a variety of styles of headdress, and will create a design to complement the bouquet. The only hazard with a fresh-flower headdress is that the effect will be spoiled if the flowers are disturbed when the headdress is being positioned on the bride's head. The bride must also take care to choose flowers that will not wilt or droop too readily especially if the weather is likely to be hot.

Buttonholes and corsages

The leading men usually have a buttonhole. Many bridal couples order special corsages – small, ornate arrangements to be worn on the coat – for their mothers. If the budget will allow, the couple may decide to provide buttonholes for all their guests.

COUNTING THE COST

A bride or her mother should not underestimate the cost of bouquets, posies and flower arrangements. The final cost could be prohibitive and out be of proportion with the total budget for the wedding. Prices will vary depending on the size and rarity of the blooms.

Deciding who pays for the flowers

According to *Debrett's Book of Etiquette*, the groom pays for his bride's bouquet and her father foots the bill for the rest. Some grooms pay for all the flowers, and so do some bride's fathers. It is up to the couple to sort out an arrangement which best suits them.

Flowers checklist – planning

- Decide on the style of flower arrangements and bouquets to suit the wedding
- Check with clergyman or the register office whether personal flowers are permitted
- Discuss with the florist the most suitable flowers for the design of the bouquet, posies, headdresses, church and reception displays
- Order the flowers two months in advance to allow for deliveries and composition at the florist
- Arrange delivery of flower arrangements the day before the wedding

Seasonal guide to flowers

Some flowers are available all year round, others can only be acquired at specific times of the year, and a limited number of flowers can be bought even when they are out of season – usually at greatly-inflated prices, however!

Winter flowers
Carnation
Chrysanthe mum
Freesia
Forsythia
Gypsophila
Gentian
Iris
Lily
Orchid
Rose
Stephanotis
Snowdrop
Winter jasmine

Spring flowers
Azalea
Apple blossom
Broom
Bluebell
Carnation
Cherry blossom
Chrysanthemum
Clematis
Camellia
Daffodil
Daisy
Forsythia
Freesia
Gladioli
Honeysuckle
Iris
Jasmine
Lilac
Lily
Mimosa
Orchid
Polyanthus
Rhododendron
Stephanotis
Tulip

Summer flowers
Aster
Azalea
Carnation
Cornflower
Chrysanthemum
Delphinium
Daisy
Freesia
Fuchsia
Gladioli
Hollyhock
Heather
Iris
Jasmine
Lilac
Lily
Lily-of-the-valley
Lupin
Marigold
Orchid
Peony
Rose
Rhododendron
Stock
Sweet Pea
Sweet William
Tiger Lily

Autumn flowers
Chrysanthemum
Daisy
Dahlia
Freesia
Gladioli
Gypsophila
Iris
Lily
Morning-glory
Orchid
Rose

FLORAL TRADITIONS AND CUSTOMS

Flowers have been an integral part of wedding ceremonies since at least Roman times, when both bride and groom wore floral garlands. The tradition of the flower girl, strewing rose petals along the aisle of the church, probably dates from the Middle Ages.

The bride's bouquet

In addition to considering the colour scheme and personal preference, some brides take into account the symbolism associated with some flowers when selecting their bouquet arrangement. The table (opposite) lists the most popular flowers, together with their hidden messages.

Orange blossoms are a traditional flower to include; to some they symbolize that the purity of the bride equals her loveliness. Because the tree from which they come is evergreen, they are also thought to symbolize the everlasting nature of the newlyweds' love for each other.

Another tradition is to have knots at the end of the bouquet ribbons; these 'lover's knots' symbolize unity, and each one represents a good wish for the couple.

Flowers for men

Men usually only wear a single flower in their buttonhole, if any at all. This is rooted in a tradition of wedding 'favours', usually made of ribbon and given to all guests at the wedding. Men in the 1700s sometimes wore satin bows; today the 'favour' is most likely to be a single white carnation, although in some places, such as the United States, the groom might wear a small version of the bridal bouquet – one or two flowers and some foliage, perhaps – in the buttonhole of his jacket.

Flower symbolism

Popular flowers which are traditionally associated with particular emotions or messages.

Flower	Hidden message
Carnation	fascination
Chrysanthemum	truth
Daffodil	regard
Daisy	innocence
Fern	fascination
Flowering almond	hope
Forget-me-not	remembrance
Heliotrope	devotion
Honeysuckle	generosity
Hyacinth	loveliness
Ivy	fidelity
Iris	flame
Japonica	loveliness
Jasmine	amiability
Lemon blossom	fidelity in love
Lilac	youthful innocence
Lily	majesty
Lily-of-the-valley	return of happiness
Magnolia	perseverance
Maidenhair	discretion
Mimosa	sensitivity
Orange blossom	purity
Peach blossom	captive
Rose	love
Sweetpea	pleasure
Tulip	love
Veronica	fidelity
Violet	faithfulness

Flowers checklist – on the day
Bride's flowers
- Are there any favourite flowers I want included?
- If so, are they available at this time of year?
- Do I want to include any flowers because of their sentimental value?
- What colour flowers do I want?
- Do I need fresh flowers for either my hair or my headdress?
- How much money do I have available to spend on flowers?
- How much notice do I need to give the florist?
- Will the flowers be delivered, or do I have to collect them?

Attendant's flowers
- What style of bouquet should the bridesmaids carry?
- Should they be the same colour as my own bouquet?
- How many buttonholes do we need, and what colour should they be?
- Who will collect them and when, or will they be delivered?
- Has someone been asked to hand them out?
- Should we order flowers for the mothers of both the bride and the groom?

Reception flowers
- If we hold the reception at an hotel or a restaurant, will the flowers be their responsibility, or that of the caterer (if we decide to use one)?
- How much will the reception flowers cost?
- What floral arrangements do we want?
- Do we want any extra flowers for decorating either the wedding cake or the tables?

10. Arranging the photography

CHOOSING A PHOTOGRAPHER
'Snaps' from family and friends

Unless the bride and groom really do not mind about quality and composition of their wedding photographs, even preferring the informality of 'snaps', then it is unwise to rely on relatives and friends collectively to provide a range of photographs of the day. However good their cameras, few people have the expertise to compose a photograph and, indeed, it would be unfair to expect guests to take the responsibility. Encourage them to take their own personal favourite scenes and pass on the results, but the real photographic record of the day should be taken by a professional.

Finding a professional photographer

On recommendation

Recommendation is always a sure sign that a photographer is of the standard expected. If other friends or relatives have used a particular individual or firm, then evidence of competence is readily available. An accurate guide to cost is also important. But if no one known to the couple or their family and friends is able to recommend a photographer, then the couple will be faced with finding a good one themselves.

Classified directory and advertisements

Most areas have good, local photographers whose addresses can be found in a classified directory. Many advertise in the local press or may have high street premises. The couple can start off by choosing three or four they like the sound or look of, either from the services they advertise or the display in their shop window. Many photographers have a brochure prepared which sets out their full range of services and the cost. Those who specialize in weddings often quote package deals, which include specified numbers of prints plus an album. The couple should then visit each photographer personally and ask to see examples of their work.

Deciding on a budget

The couple need to decide on what they are prepared to pay for photographs and how many they want. The quality of the album is a significant factor, because many luxurious designs are very expensive, often eclipsing the cost of the prints. The couple might also want albums for their respective parents (a good thank-you present and an excellent memento), as well as extra prints for relatives and friends.

WHAT TO LOOK FOR

The photographer's availability

A final deciding factor on a couple's choice of photographer is his availability for the day. Many photographers are booked up well in advance, so the couple should make arrangements a minimum of three months before the date of the wedding and reception or, preferably, as soon as the date has been agreed.

Discussing needs and arrangements

Once they have a firm idea of their requirements, the bride and groom can assess whether a photographer can provide them with their needs. Possibly one of the

packages on offer will fit the bill; but if not, it is always
worth discussing with a photographer the differences
between his packages and what is wanted, because an
individual arrangement could be made.

Pricing structures

Different photographers have different pricing
structures. Some charge an hourly rate, then a lower
price per print; others charge only for the prints.
Obviously, the photographer's hourly rate will have
been included in this. It is important that the couple has
decided on the number of photographs they will need
on the day, as this will affect their choice of pricing
structure. The following example indicates how
important this choice is.

Examples

1 The couple may want 25 photographs, taken over a
3-hour period, perhaps of the ceremony and part of the
reception up to the cutting of the cake. Photographer 1
(Ph 1) charges an hourly rate (e.g. £20 an hour) and for
the prints. Photographer 2 (Ph 2) charges only for the
prints. The resulting costs might be

	Hourly rate (£)	Price per print (£)	Total cost
Ph 1	20 (x 3)	7	(20 x 3) + (25 x 7) = £235
Ph 2	—	10	25 x 10 = £250

2 The couple wants 40 photographs, taken over an
8-hour period, perhaps from the time the bride puts on
her dress to the time the bridal couple leaves the
reception. See overleaf for the resulting costs.

	Hourly rate (£)	Price per print (£)	Total cost
Ph 1	20 (x 8)	7	(20 x 8) + (40 x 7) =**£440**
Ph 2	—	10	40 x 10 = **£400**

Hidden costs

Viewing the proofs

In addition, different photographers have different
procedures for the viewing of proofs. Some are even
able to offer them late at the reception (if the
assignment has ended perhaps with the cutting of the
cake), others send them on about a week after the
ceremony. Some charge for proofs if not enough prints
are ordered, so the couple should check the minimum
order and see if it fits in with their requirements. If not,
the charge for proofs – usually a one-off and not a price
per print – should be added to the costs to see if the
total still comes within the budget.

Value added tax

The couple should remember that photographers'
charges are usually exclusive of VAT. So they should
take into account the current rate of VAT, when
assessing costs, as it may make a considerable
difference to the final expenditure.

Checking the quality

Before the bride and groom decide on a photographer,
for reasons of cost, they should see examples of his or
her work. If they are approaching a large firm with
several photographers, they should ask to see work
done by the individual assigned to their wedding, not
just the anonymous pictures proffered in a company
brochure.

ORDER OF PHOTOGRAPHY
Preliminary discussions

Either at the time of booking or in the week prior to the wedding, the bride and groom should discuss with the photographer *in person* (not the receptionist or manager at the shop) the subject of each photograph. This should then be confirmed in writing, as it can avoid distressing arguments should all not go to plan.

Popular subjects and order of photographs

If the number of photographs required is small, perhaps 20, then the compositions below are usually the ones favoured by the bridal couple.

1 Bride at her house (alone)
2 Bride with father
3 Groom and best man outside church or register office
4 Bride with bridesmaids (same)
5 Bride and father entering church or register office
6 Bride and groom signing the register
7 Bride and groom at the church or register office door
8 Bride and groom with bridesmaids and best man
9 Bride and groom with her parents
10 Bride and groom with his parents
11 Bride and groom with bridesmaids, best man and her parents
12 Bride and groom with bridesmaids, best man and his parents
13 Bride and groom with all attendants, both sets of parents and respective wider families
14 The whole wedding party

15 Bride and groom alone, perhaps in romantic pose, looking at the ring(s)
16 Bride and groom leaving for the reception
17 Bride and groom arriving at the reception
18 The top table
19 Cutting the cake
20 Bride and groom leaving the reception

PHOTOGRAPHING THE CEREMONY

Many couples wish the ceremony itself to be recorded, but before they make any arrangements with the photographer, they should ask the permission of the clergyman or registrar. Some, particularly clergymen, have strict views on what is really an intrusion into a solemn rite, and will refuse outright. This is his prerogative and the couple must respect that. Others have no objection to photographs in their churches or offices, provided no lights or flashes are used, or provided (in some cases) the actual marriage itself is not photographed. It is worth finding out exactly what is allowed, to avoid conflict or bad feeling on the day.

VIDEO RECORDINGS

This is an increasingly popular way of recording the wedding day. Several video production companies specialize in weddings, and if the couple would like to consider this 'live' memento of their big day, they should approach the film-makers exactly as they would the photographer. Relatives and friends with modern compact camcorders could be enlisted, although the same risk of uneven quality exists as it does with amateur photography. There is no guarantee of how any video recording will turn out. With professional film-

makers, as with photographers, they have their
reputation to protect, and are also insured.

Advantage of video

One advantage of having a video of the wedding day is
that the recording is immediate, and could add to the
evening's entertainment if shown to the guests.

Photography checklist

- Decide on the content and extent of your wedding
  photograph album, and how much you want to pay
  for it
- Select a local photographer
- If choosing from advertisements, ask to see the price
  list and samples of work
- Check for any hidden costs, e.g. charges for proofs,
  and if VAT is inclusive or exclusive
- If using a large firm, check the availability of the
  photographer you want, and ask to see samples of
  his or her own work, not just the company brochure
- About a week before the ceremony, discuss with
  the photographer, *in person*, the order of
  photographs and confirm it in writing
- Check with the clergyman or registrar whether
  photography is allowed in the church or register
  office
- If you opt for having your wedding video-recorded,
  follow the same pattern as for a photographer
- Ask whether the video will be available later on at the
  reception so you can organize viewing (if required)

11. Going away

Before the day

BOOKING AHEAD

The couple should make honeymoon plans, including
booking time off work, as soon as the wedding date is
set. This will prevent disappointment. Early booking is
advisable because of all the other arrangements that
need to be taken into account.

Planning and budgeting

As the honeymoon is part of the whole event, it will
need careful planning – and budgeting. It is likely to be
the most expensive item next to the reception, so the
bridal couple should decide at the outset how much
they can – or are prepared to – spend on a holiday. This
is usually the deciding factor on choice of destination.
As the honeymoon is so special, the couple might
choose to spend more than they would normally and so
opt for an exotic destination, such as the Far East,
which they are unlikely to visit again.

Booking flights

When booking flights, a couple should consider the
time and expected duration of the reception. If they
plan to leave from an afternoon reception, they should
check there is plenty of time between their expected
departure from the reception and the time they have to
check in at the airport. Allowances should be made for
heavy traffic, road congestion or train delays. If
possible, a 'dummy run' could be made to ensure that
sufficient time has been allowed.

If the timings are not suitable, the couple could spend their first night in a nearby hotel so they can take their time in getting to the airport for a flight the following day. In this instance, they might run to the expense of a bridal suite as it would be just for one night.

WHERE TO GO
Deciding factors
Even if their choice of holiday spot is near home, the weather is likely to be a deciding factor. European destinations which offer sun, sea and a relaxing atmosphere are therefore popular, while British resorts or places of interest are attractive because of price.

Types of honeymoon
A honeymoon, however, does not have to be one of sun-soaked days and romantic nights by a moonlit sea. It all depends on the couple's interests. A tour of historic cities might fit their idea of a dream holiday, or perhaps even one that includes leisure pursuits such as pony trekking, skiing or canoeing.

Honeymoon suite
Next, the couple should decide whether their honeymoon is meant to publicize their newlywed status – do they book the bridal suite or just an ordinary room and keep their secret? If they want to tell the world, they should inform the tour operator or hotel. Many have special arrangements for newlyweds, from roses and champagne on arrival to sumptuous suites with four-poster beds. All this is likely to be at a price, so extra costs should be checked and agreed to avoid the nasty surprise of a much higher bill at the end of the holiday.

DOCUMENTS AND INJECTIONS
Documents
Any holiday outside Britain requires a valid passport
and possibly a visa – too often overlooked in the welter
of other preparations. Therefore the couple should
attend to these as soon as they know they are going out
of the country. A passport is not required for the
Channel Islands, the Isle of Man, Northern Ireland and
the Irish Republic.
Injections
Some exotic holidays entail several inoculations
against diseases prevalent in those parts, and they have
to be given some weeks before the trip to be effective.

PASSPORT PROCEDURES
If the honeymoon is abroad, the couple should ensure
they have valid passports. The one-year British
Visitor's Passport, valid for travel to Western Europe, is
being abolished from 1 January 1996 (from 1 October
1995 for travellers to Spain). It may be preferable to
obtain a standard, 10-year passport. All necessary
forms can be obtained at major post offices.
Applying for a full passport
Form A should be filled out and posted to the
recommended regional passport office at least a month
before the new passport is needed. If everything is in
order, it will arrive within three weeks even at the
busiest time of the year.
The bride's passport
If the bride wants her passport in her married name, she
must either obtain a new passport (as detailed above) or
amend her existing one (using Form C). In both cases,
she will also need to obtain Forms PD1 and PD2; the

latter must be completed by the clergyman or registrar.
The new or amended passport will be valid from the
date of the wedding but, be warned, an amended
passport cannot be used before the date of the
ceremony. If a visa is required, check with the relevant
embassy regarding its policy on post-dated passports.
The bride should make sure her plane ticket, traveller's
cheques, and so on, are made out in the same name as
on the passport, should she need to prove her identity.

INSURANCE
Everyone hopes the honeymoon will go perfectly to
plan, but accidents can happen. So it is wise to arrange
insurance to cover all eventualities, from injury and
loss of property to sickness and delay. Most holiday
companies have insurance included in their packages. If
not, the couple's insurance broker can arrange a policy
to suit their requirements with very little trouble.

PAYING FOR THE HONEYMOON
Traditionally, the groom pays for the honeymoon, and
he may wish to do so in advance (which most tour
operators insist on) or to settle later. One advantage of
paying in advance is that any tickets are sent on
immediately, relieving the couple of any anxiety on that
score. On the day, the best man should be entrusted
with the care of passports, tickets and other travel
documents – such as foreign currency – which he keeps
until just before the couple is due to leave the reception.

GOING AWAY CLOTHES
The honeymoon, of course, requires holiday clothing,
none of which is so important as the bride's 'going
away outfit'. Usually this is something special which

she changes into from her wedding dress in order to leave the reception. Some thought should be given to the honeymoon destination when choosing an outfit. Something chic made from fragile material, for example, will not look so attractive after a 12-hour flight to a distant holiday spot.

On the day

LEAVING THE RECEPTION

When it is time to leave the reception, the bride and groom change into their going away clothes, and the bride throws her bouquet into the crowd. Tradition has it that whichever (female) guest catches it will be the next bride. Tradition also holds that the honeymoon destination is a well-kept secret. This might also apply to the whereabouts of the groom's car, if the couple does not want it decorated in the time-honoured fashion with tin cans, shaving foam and streamers.

The role of the best man

It is the best man's responsibility to make sure the couple's car is ready for them to leave promptly. He should hand over all tickets and documents to the groom before waving them off on their journey. After the newlyweds have gone, the reception or party may continue for some hours, but it will be the best man's duty to end the celebrations, to make sure everyone has transport home, and to take care of the groom's discarded wedding clothes and any wedding presents given to the couple on the day.

After the day

COMING HOME

Tradition has it that a man carry his bride over the threshold of their new home. He may do this anyway, regardless of where they are living, or save up the moment until they do have a home of their own. Whatever they decide, the newly married couple will return from honeymoon relaxed, after the months of preparations and the excitement of their wedding day, and ready to begin their new life together.

Going away checklist

- Decide on the type of honeymoon you want and how much you are prepared to spend
- Plan well in advance and book the time off work as early as possible
- Make reservations as soon as possible
- Check which documents are required for the trip (passport and visa, for example)
- Check whether inoculation against specific diseases is required for your destination and make sure you obtain these in good time for them to be effective while you are away
- Check times of flights and that you will have time to make them after leaving the reception
- If not, consider staying somewhere en route for the first night of the honeymoon
- Choose going away outfits appropriate to the holiday destination you have chosen
- Entrust the best man with all documents on the day to save worry

Thankyous

When you return from honeymoon there will be lots to sort out, but don't neglect any extra thankyous that are needed. Of course there will probably be quite a few thankyou notes for wedding presents that arrived on the day itself and couldn't be incorporated into the pre-wedding arrangements, but there may also be some people to whom you want to say a special thankyou. For instance, both sets of parents would no doubt appreciate written appreciation of their help and support through the hectic wedding planning, and on the actual day itself. You might even care to send a bouquet or a little present to them. It might also be a good idea to send a written thankyou to your bridesmaids, the best man and any other attendants. To accompany these thankyou notes, you may consider enclosing a good enlargement of one of your best wedding photographs, perhaps in a special frame, so that they could put them in a position of prominence in their homes as a reminder of the happy occasion! There will probably also be other people you will want to thank formally – caterers, photographers, flower arrangers, people who helped at an evening party, car drivers, ushers, colleagues from work who clubbed together for a special present, etc. It will make everyone feel that their hard work was appreciated if you can find the time to drop them a note or make a quick telephone call.

People we need to say thankyou to	Phone call or letter?	Done (date)

12. The bride

Role and responsibilities
Before the day: preparations

● With the groom, thinks about and sets the date
● With the groom, arranges the ceremony
● With her mother, arranges the reception
● Works towards looking good on the day
● Attends the wedding rehearsal
● Packs and prepares for the honeymoon

Before the day: the wedding dress

● Chooses colour, length and style
● Decides whether to hire, make or buy the dress
● Attends fittings
● Chooses the headdress and train (if having one)
● Chooses the accessories
● Chooses the bridesmaids' outfits and accessories

On the day: before the ceremony

● Makes sure her honeymoon luggage is taken to the reception venue
● Ensures the best man collects the service sheets
● Leaves in good time for the ceremony

On the day: the ceremony

● Signs the register
● With the groom, heads the recessional out of the church

On the day: at the reception

● Takes part in receiving the guests
● With the groom, leaves for the honeymoon

Before the day: preparations

If the wedding is to be paid for by the bride's parents, then most of the arrangements may be taken over by the bride's mother (see pp. 236-48). These will include the reception and catering (see pp. 106-43), the flowers (see pp. 166-76) and photographer (see pp. 177–83), and may include organizing the purchase, hire or making of the wedding dress (see pp. 198-208) and bridesmaids' dresses (see pp. 278–80). But all this cannot take place until the bride has completed her most important task – setting the date. Although the decision is made by both of the bridal couple, the bride should have the casting vote because of her more prominent role in the proceedings.

SETTING THE DATE
There are several important things to be considered when setting the date. First, the wedding will have to be at a time when, as well as the bridal couple, the best man, ushers and bridesmaids can attend, as well as important relatives and friends. Seasons and weather will also have to be taken into account.

Menstrual cycle
The wedding day is not just a show, but the start of a marriage. Depending on the importance of consummation on the wedding night – and in many religions, this is crucial to the harmony of the whole event – the bride will want to make sure that all will be well on the day. This means calculating a date that will not coincide with her menstrual cycle. Even if such a coincidence will not worry a couple unduly, the bride

will probably not feel her best at this time because of
related symptoms, for example, headaches, stomach
cramps, backache or tension.

Family planning

If such a coincidence cannot be avoided – restrictions
on time off from work, or an irregular cycle upsetting
careful calculations, for example – then the bride
should see her doctor at least three months before the
wedding day to explain the situation.

This will give her doctor time to assess the problem,
examine the bride for medical suitability and prescribe
hormonal treatment by which the date of menstruation
can be regulated. Very often, the bride will have
thought of visiting her doctor or family planning clinic
anyway to prepare for her new role. Again, this should
be done at least three months before the wedding.

ARRANGING THE CEREMONY

Once the date is set, the bride and her groom should
contact the clergyman of the church in which they wish
to be married (see 'Church weddings', pp. 90–5) or the
superintendent registrar for their area (see 'Register
office weddings', p. 81) if the wedding is to take place
in a register office.

FALLING ILL

One worry a bride could well do without is falling ill
and being unable to go through with the wedding.
Unfortunately, illness does not discriminate and often
cannot be avoided. However, the bride can take
precautions by avoiding people with, particularly, viral
infections up to a month before the wedding. Most of
these infections have a two- or three-week incubation

period, and an infection contracted early on could
manifest its unpleasant symptoms at just the wrong
time.

Relieving illness

If the bride does become ill in the week before her
wedding, she should visit her doctor who may be able
to prescribe a relieving remedy which will ensure she
will feel much better on the day. Serious or infectious
illness is a different matter, and cancellation of the
wedding will depend on individual circumstances.

MAKE-UP AND APPEARANCE
Make-up

A bride may opt to have her face professionally made
up for her wedding, especially if she is not used to
wearing much make-up. If so, she should visit several
beauticians to find the most suitable. Some will be able
to visit the bride's house on the day, others will only
offer a treatment on their premises. Whatever the
arrangements, the bride should discuss with the chosen
beautician the colour scheme of her headdress and
flowers, so the right choice of make-up can be made.
Most brides, however, will want to do their own make-
up, seeing this as an essential part of creating their own
beautiful image for their big day. Many will have a
tried and tested 'best look', and so will be confident of
their appearance. Others may be unused to make-up, or
may just want to experiment with a different look.
However, even though she has a clear idea of how she
wants to look, the bride should always seek objective
advice, possibly from a trusted friend or relative. Many
shop demonstrators can be very helpful, but the bride

should remember that their first priority is to sell cosmetics, not to perfect the bride's looks.

Weight-watching

Apart from making decisions about menus, photographers and flowers, the bride will be occupying herself mainly with the design and choice of wedding dress and going-away outfit in the months before the wedding. She will be trying on several versions, and possibly having alterations made to her final choice to ensure a correct fit. It is therefore important that she remain the same weight and shape from the time these fittings take place – often two or three months before the wedding – to the day itself.

Diet

A balanced diet is essential, as are regular meals. The excitement and tensions created by the preparations can make eating seem an irrelevance, and so many brides actually lose, rather than gain, weight in the run-up to their wedding. Increased slimness may sound attractive, but will not look it if the wedding dress is ill-fitting on the day. Conversely, an overweight bride can use this opportunity of not feeling like eating to slim down to her dream weight so she looks her very best on the day.

Looking good and keeping fit

To help her keep in trim, a bride may embark on an exercise régime in the months before her wedding. A weekly massage, work-out, keep-fit or yoga class, plus sauna or facial, will all help to boost a healthy appearance. Some brides may even entertain the idea of taking a sun-bed course so they look healthily tanned on the day. This option is attractive if the wedding is in high summer or the honeymoon is somewhere hot.

Hairstyle

Many brides are tempted to try a special hairstyle to
make themselves extra-glamorous on their wedding
day. If a bride has long hair, she may experiment with
different styles well before the wedding to see which
suits her – and her wedding ensemble – best. If a new
style necessitates the bride's hair being cut, then she
should think about trying this out at least six months in
advance. This way, if the experiment is a failure, then
she has time to grow her hair sufficiently long to have it
restyled.

Asking the hairdresser's advice

A reputable hairdresser will be able to show brochures
of various styles. He or she will advise a bride which
are most suitable, especially if the bride takes along her
headdress so the hairdresser has a better idea of the
finished look.

Just before the wedding

Once the decision has been made, the bride should aim
to have her hair cut at least two weeks before the
wedding to allow it to settle into its new style, then
make a final appointment on the day before – or on the
day itself – to have her hair professionally finished so it
looks its very best. Some hairdressers will visit the
bride's house on the morning of the wedding to arrange
her headdress. It is worth finding this out before
engaging a particular hairdresser if this attention is
wanted on the day.

Beautiful hands

Everyone will want to see the bride's wedding ring in
place on her hand, and so it is worth her taking time to
condition her hands before the wedding day. A

manicure may not be necessary, but the bride should ensure her nails are clean and well shaped. If the bride has long nails and is in the habit of painting them, she should clean off all old polish a few days before the wedding and apply a conditioner. Then on the day, she should leave plenty of time to apply a new coat of polish ready for the ceremony. Finally, regular application of a good moisturizer night and morning will give the skin a soft appearance.

Before the day: the wedding dress

TRADITIONS ABOUT COLOUR

The white wedding dress

The true white wedding with all its accoutrements is only as old as the Victorian era, though white as the bridal colour was a Greek tradition. In the distant past, white symbolized joy; now it is more often associated with chastity and virginity, which is why brides in second marriages traditionally don't wear pure white, but cream and other off-white colours (although of course that, like many traditions, is nowadays less often followed than in the past).

Ancient and more recent colour traditions

Roman brides wore yellow veils; for the Chinese, red is the colour of tradition.

For much of the first half of this century, silver (in the form of embroidery or trim) became the rage for wedding dresses among royal and non-royal brides alike. It coincided briefly with a short-lived attempt to remove the superstitious stigma surrounding the colour black, which for a short time was used in bridal hats,

trims and even dresses. Silver is still sometimes used
for bridal accessories.

Blue, sometimes thought of as a symbol of constancy,
also plays a part in the traditional bride's outfit,
according to the well-known rhyme:

> *Something old, something new,*
> *Something borrowed, something blue.*

The 'old' was sometimes an old garter donated by a
happily married woman as a way of bestowing
happiness on the new bride. Sometimes this rhyme
includes a line referring to a sixpence in the bride's
shoe; some contemporary brides keep with this tradition
by placing a penny in the bottom of one shoe for the
ceremony.

Colour associations

Another well-known rhyme associates a moral or
message with each of several common colours:

> *Married in white*
> *You have chosen aright.*
> *Married in green,*
> *Ashamed to be seen.*
> *Married in grey,*
> *You'll go far away.*
> *Married in red,*
> *You'll wish yourself dead.*
> *Married in blue,*
> *Love ever true.*
> *Married in yellow,*
> *Ashamed of your fellow.*
> *Married in black,*

You'll wish yourself back.
Married in pink,
Your spirits will sink.

CHOOSING THE COLOUR

Any first-time bride may wear white, even if she is
marrying in a register office. It is her choice. But, she
may choose not to wear white. Perhaps she may feel
that the colour is too harsh for her complexion, and a
softer shade would be more flattering. Whatever the
reason, there is no limit to the colour she may choose,
although the more lurid colours, such as red, orange
and purple, might look too frivolous for a serious
occasion.

Late starters and second timers

Those women who are marrying late in life or for the
second time usually opt for an alternative to white
when choosing their dress. They may feel that white
does not suit their status or their age. Favourite
alternatives are any of the near-whites – oyster, ivory,
cream or magnolia – or one of the pastel colours.

CHOOSING THE LENGTH

Length of dress is a matter of choice, too. The
'traditional' long, flowing extravagance of silky fabric,
lace and ribbons is still a firm favourite, but a bride
who opts for a simple knee-length design will look
every bit as stunning if the dress suits her. Brides who
are marrying in a register office may feel that a long
dress with train and veil might look too fussy for the
rather austere surroundings, but many do wear the full
regalia without looking out of place.

CHOOSING THE STYLE

A dress may look beautiful on the rack, or on the pattern packet, but do nothing for the wearer just because it is the wrong style. Perhaps the skirt is too full for the bride's height, or the bodice too close-fitting for her weight, or the decorations too fussy for her looks. Most importantly, the neckline may be too deep for her figure or for the approval of the clergyman or registrar. In some churches, the bridal couple may spend a considerable time on their knees in front of the clergyman, who will disapprove of an over-exposed cleavage as inappropriate for the occasion.

Deciding to have a train

The bride should consider the wisdom of having a train. A glorious length of material stretching yards behind the bride looks breathtaking, but is it practical? The bride should not underestimate the weight or bulk of such a train, and must consider who will carry it – certainly not child bridesmaids – and what it will look like after it has been bundled up into the bridal car on the way to the church or register office. A shorter train, perhaps trailing just a few feet in length, would look just as effective and be much more manageable.

TO BUY OR NOT TO BUY?

The purchase of a wedding dress will have been one of the priorities when the bride's parents – or the bridal couple themselves – have budgeted for the whole occasion. However, circumstances may bring them round to the idea that buying is not the best policy. Perhaps the sort of dress the bride wants is far beyond her means, or she feels that, once worn, the dress

becomes a burden to be kept forever and of no real use.
(Few married women can bring themselves to throw
away their wedding dress).

Hiring the dress

In such cases, the bride may choose to hire her special
dress. There are plenty of hire shops, both specialist
and within large fashion stores, which have an
extensive range to suit all pockets. If the bride finds
what she wants here, she should check certain details
before concluding the transaction.

Important questions to ask

● Will the dress be available on the day?
● Will the previous wearer have it back in time for it to
  be cleaned and ready for her to collect?
● What alternatives are there if the dress is damaged
  or otherwise unavailable?
● Does the cost cover hire for the day, or for a 24-
  hour period?
● Does the dress have to be cleaned before it is
  returned?
● Can the dress be insured against damage during
  the period of hire?

These points are a formality to the professional hirer,
but they should be checked just the same.

Making the dress

A third choice awaits the bride who does not find the
dress she wants either in the bridal or hire shop: she
may have her dress made or make it herself. The bride
may like the idea of walking down the aisle in her own
creation, but she should think seriously about her
expertise before embarking on a very costly exercise.

The bride as dressmaker

Unless she is choosing a very simple, straightforward design in an easy-to-work-with fabric, the dressmaker-bride will have to contend with a complicated pattern using perhaps two or three delicate fabrics, perhaps also lace. If she is experienced, then she should have no problem, but it is not worth a novice risking ruining costly fabric with inaccurate measuring, poor cutting or uneven stitching. It may not show on the day, but she may think it does, and that is what matters.

Employing a professional dressmaker

Far better to choose a pattern and material (do not buy until advised of the correct amount) and employ a professional dressmaker. She will incorporate all the bride's individual preferences in the pattern, will give her several fittings, and may even offer to visit her on the wedding day to make any last-minute alterations. All this will be for a price, of course, which the bride should settle before the work starts.

Buying 'off the peg'

Specialist bridal shops and department stores keep dozens of styles in a range of sizes, and most offer a fitting and alteration service at a small extra cost.

Having a second opinion

When going out to try on a dress, the bride should take someone with her who can make an objective judgement. However encircling the shop's mirrors, the bride herself cannot get a complete picture of herself. Her mother is the obvious choice, but if their taste in styles is too diverse, a good friend's advice would probably be more productive.

Trying on the dress

The bride should wear similar underwear and shoes (especially the same height of heel) to those she proposes to wear on the day. This way, she will know if the dress is the correct fit and the correct length.

Important points to consider
- Is it tight?
- Does the neckline flatter her?
- Can she move her arms freely?
- Does it look just as pretty from the back? (For most of the ceremony, this is the view the guests will have of the dress.)
- Does the design *suit* her?

The fitting

When the bride has tried on the dress she wants, she should ask the shop's professional fitter to examine the fit for possible alterations. The fitter will spot any imperfections and discuss it with the bride. Upon agreement, she will make the adjustments there and then with pins, or even tacking cotton. She then takes the dress and assigns it to the workroom, which is usually behind the scenes at most shops, although some that are short of space will have their workroom elsewhere. Alterations take time, especially if the shop is busy, so the bride should allow at least three weeks for her dress to be ready. This time would include any last-minute alterations.

Looking after the dress

When the dress is ready, most shops are careful to pack the garment in tissue to avoid creasing. However, once home, the dress should be unpacked and hung up on a hanger so that any creases can be smoothed out. It is very rare that a dress is so crumpled that it needs ironing; but if it is the case, great care must be taken, following the shop's or manufacturer's instructions.

FINISHING TOUCHES

Once all the basic decisions have been made about the colour, length, and style of your dress, you might also consider the variety of ways in which you can make the garment special, and personal, to yourself. Some finishing touches are discussed (below), but there are many more combinations of colour and effect which can be achieved if you have the time and inclination.

Floral motifs

Tiny coloured flowers can be dotted over the whole of the dress, or just over the hemline or the sleeves, to achieve a decorative effect. Or, larger flowers can be made out of fabric and then appliqued to the dress.

Lace, net and embroidery

Transparent lace can be used as a bodice, and also as sleeve material, over a more opaque fabric. Lace is suitable for both necklines and inset panels, whereas net placed (in a layered form) over the main fabric of the dress can produce an 'ethereal' look. Embroidery can be used to decorate any part of the dress.

Ribbons, ruffles and flounces

Ribbons can be used to tie in bows on sleeves and flounces, and also as sashes. Ruffles of lace or fabric can decorate sleeves, necklines, hemlines or flounces. (Flounces are real or pretend gatherings of the fabric, usually decorated with a bow.)

Sashes, tucks and trains

Sashes made from any material can be used to nip in
the waist, and also to neaten the waistline. Small or
large tucks can be made in the fabric of the skirt, bodice
or sleeve. Trains, which are extensions of the fabric at
the back of the skirt, are generally reserved for more
formal occasions.

PRESERVING YOUR WEDDING DRESS

Some specialist companies offer a service for treating
wedding dresses for long-term storage. The process –
after the actual treatment, the gown is sealed in an
airtight container – protects the fabric of the dress from
any kind of deterioration, including discoloration, rot,
rust damage, and even attacks by insects.

CHOOSING THE HEADDRESS

Tiaras

Once, the conventional headdress for a bride in
traditional white was some sort of tiara, whether with
real or paste gems. While some brides still make this
choice today, the fashion is to opt for a more natural
look, perhaps with flowers.

Real-flower headdresses

Real-flower headdresses are not unusual, and florists
who offer a bridal flower service will have several
designs from which to choose. The headdress is usually
made up with the same variety of flowers as the bride's
bouquet and is delivered on the wedding morning.

Fabric-flower headdresses

Fabric flowers may not be quite as effective, but a bride
with many other worries on her mind would be more

sure of their condition on the day. Most bridal shops or departments have an extensive range of fabric flower headdresses in a variety of colour schemes which will match the chosen colours of, say, the bouquet. It is best to try on a selection of headdresses with the wedding dress to make sure the designs are complementary.

The veil

Although not compulsory, the veil is the most symbolic item of the bride's attire. In most religious ceremonies, the bride comes to her future husband with her face covered. She (or the chief bridesmaid) lifts back the veil as the ceremony begins, and she becomes a married woman with her face uncovered. Veils can also be worn at a register office wedding.

Veil length

The bride can choose from several lengths of veil, from a short, shoulder-length version to a long, flowing mist of voile which stretches back as far as her train. Whichever she selects, it should be completely in keeping with the dress and, above all, manageable.

Wearing a hat

The bride may prefer a hat to complete her ensemble. This may be a wise choice if her dress is not especially a wedding dress, or is in a colour other than white or near white. A hat also means the bride does not have to wear a veil. She should check with the clergyman (if having a church wedding) if this offends any church custom, although many hats have a short veil over the eyes which would probably suffice.

Carrying a prayer book

By custom, brides who wear hats do not carry flowers, but many opt for a prayer book instead of a bouquet

whether they wear a hat or a headdress, so a bride
without a bouquet would not necessarily look out of
place.

ACCESSORIES

Personalizing a bought wedding dress is an inexpensive
way for a bride to be unique on her big day.
Haberdashery departments or specialist needlework
shops often stock lace or fabric flowers, horse-shoes or
other appropriate ornaments that can be sewn onto the
dress, perhaps around the neck, waist or hemline, for
effect. Silver-coloured decorations or imitation pearls
would add glitter to a plainer garment.

Something borrowed, something blue

The traditional 'something old, something new;
something borrowed, something blue' can easily be
realized in wedding dress decorations. Ideas could
include a mother's brooch, a new ornament, a bow
from a sister's wedding dress, a blue flower, or even a
blue garter.

On the day

TRADITIONS AND SUPERSTITIONS

Preparing for the ceremony

In some cultures, tradition holds that the bride should
not try on her complete wedding outfit before the day,
that she should not finish dressing until the last minute,
and that the groom should not see her (or her wedding
dress) until she appears in church. For some, these
traditions are based on superstitions that ill fortune will
befall those who break them. The superstitious also
believe that good luck will come to the bride who finds

a spider in her dress as she prepares for her wedding, but bad luck will come to one who breaks anything, such as a mirror, on the morning.

According to Hindu tradition, on her wedding day the bride performs certain rituals to prepare herself and her body, helped by women who are required to have had sons and whose husbands must still be alive. The Hindu groom is also anointed in preparation for his wedding. Among Orthodox Jews, the bride has a ritual bath to cleanse herself of any impurities before the wedding. Often the bride and groom are also expected to fast on the day of the wedding until the reception; this is another tradition associated with purity.

After the ceremony

It is meant to augur bad luck if a woman fails to remove and throw away every pin from her veil and dress when she changes out of her wedding attire.

BEFORE THE CEREMONY

There may not be much time for the bride to concentrate on getting ready on her wedding day. Last-minute arrangements may have to be made, gifts received and relatives arriving from out-of-town to be entertained (though, usually, the bride's mother will shoulder the responsibility; see p. 245). The bride should therefore have her routine planned out in advance, and have all her beauty preparations finished at least one hour before the wedding. She should also make sure her going-away outfit and honeymoon luggage is packed and that someone will take it to the reception hall for her. This will give her time to dress and pose for any pre-ceremony photographs.

Leaving in good time

Depending on the distance between her house and the church or register office, the bride and her father should leave the house in enough time to arrive almost on time. The bridesmaids and her mother will have left first, and she and her father will be the last to arrive for the ceremony. She should not arrive too early, in case all the guests have not taken their places, or too late – particularly at a register office – which may have several weddings to conduct at close intervals.

THE CEREMONY
Entering the church
If it is a church wedding, the bride enters on her father's right arm – or whoever is giving her away – and walks up the aisle followed by her attendants. At this time, her veil should be covering her face. When she reaches the front of the pews, her groom will step to her right side and her father will remain slightly behind her. She should then hand her bouquet to her chief bridesmaid or matron of honour and lift her veil.

Signing of the register and the recessional
After the exchange of vows, the bride and her groom will lead their attendants and parents into the vestry for the signing of the register and then lead the recessional down the aisle and out of the church for photographs (see 'Church weddings', pp. 101-3).

At the register office
Much the same procedure is followed in a register office wedding, but there is usually much less ceremony and very little room for processions (see 'Register office weddings', pp. 81–2 and 87).

AT THE RECEPTION
Receiving the guests
The bride and groom are usually first to leave the church or register office. They are the third pair in the receiving line after the bride's parents, and the groom's parents (see 'Arranging the reception', p. 141).

Role during the reception
The bride then takes her place at the top table, sitting to the left of her groom. Traditionally, she does not make a speech, but there is no rule to stop her if she feels she wants to thank her guests or make some important remarks. After the toasts, speeches and the cutting of the cake, she and her groom lead the floor if there is dancing.

Going away
At the appointed time, the bride should change into her going away outfit and meet her groom at the door of the reception venue, where they make their farewells to their guests. She should have her bridal bouquet with her so she can throw it into the crowd as her last gesture before departing for her honeymoon (see 'Going away', p. 188).

It is important for the bride to remember the 'photo-opportunities' implicit in her leaving of the reception. Changing into her going-away outfit not only provides the photographer with relatively new subject-matter, but also refocuses attention on the bride and her new husband as they prepare to go. A well-composed photograph of the assembled guests, and the lucky person who has caught the bridal bouquet, should provide a happy reminder of the end of the formal celebrations for years to come.

After the day

CHANGING NAME
Once the bride is back from honeymoon, she will begin
her life as a married woman. This may mean changing
her surname to that of her husband. This is purely a
matter of choice and not a legal requirement. If she
does decide to change her name, however, the new wife
should inform all relevant bodies of the change. A list
of these is given below.

Bodies to notify
- employer
- banks
- credit card companies
- insurance companies or agents
- all public utilities
- Inland Revenue
- Department of Health
- Department of Social Security (if applicable)
- Driver and Vehicle Licensing Centre
- passport office
- doctor and dentist

Bride's checklist
Before the day: preparations

- Set the date
- See the doctor about family planning or altering the
  menstrual cycle
- Choose wedding dress, accessories and going-away
  outfit
- Eat carefully; keep weight steady

- Take a beauty or health and fitness course, if wanted
- Try out new hairstyles or make-up ideas
- Take care of hands

Before the day: the wedding-dress

- Decide on colour and design of the dress
- Decide whether to buy, hire or have the dress made
- If hiring, check the cost and availability, as well as insurance against damage
- If making, only attempt it yourself if you are experienced in dressmaking. Otherwise, find a reputable dressmaker. Agree cost and services prior to placing the order
- When buying, take someone with you whose opinion you trust
- Wear similar underwear and shoes to those you intend to wear on the day, so that the dress fits and hangs correctly
- Ask the shop's professional fitter to make any necessary alterations
- Allow enough time between purchase of the dress and the wedding for alterations to be made
- Choose a style that suits you
- Avoid low necklines
- Envisage how manageable a train will be before choosing a dress that has one
- Always unpack the finished dress and hang for at least a day before the wedding so any creases will fall out
- Choose a headdress and veil which suits you and the dress
- If you choose a hat, remember the convention is that you do not hold flowers.

On the day

- Rise early and prepare hair, face and nails at least one hour before the ceremony
- Make sure honeymoon luggage and going away outfit are packed, and that someone takes them to the reception venue
- Dress (with the help of mother or chief bridesmaid)
- Leave home in good time to arrive at the church and register office at the appointed hour, or no more than a few minutes afterwards

Bride's countdown chart

Months in advance

Reception
- With your parents, obtain particulars from two or three firms of caterers and make an appointment with the one chosen
- Book the reception venue and band/disco
- Book the marquee for a reception at home, if required

Bridesmaids
- Choose the chief bridesmaid/matron of honour

Reception
- With your parents, make preliminary bookings for the venue, caterers, etc., if you have not already done so

Make-up and appearance
● Start to think about how you want to look on the day; If necessary, begin skin treatments, possibly arrange for your glasses to be replaced with contact lenses, etc.

Clothing
● Start looking for wedding outfits (or for fabric), for yourself and your attendants. Place special orders for unusual/ornate outfits
● If the dresses are to be made, buy the fabric and begin now. If it is to be a dressmaker that makes it, take her the fabric and arrange for everyone concerned to be measured

Reception
● With your parents and the caterers, decide on the menu
● Either start to make the wedding cake or order it

Music
● Make a firm booking with the organist/musicians

Stationery
● With your parents, order the stationery: wedding invitations, order of service sheets, place cards, etc.

Clothing
- Organize fittings and alterations of your wedding dress
- Choose the dresses and accessories for the bridesmaids
- Shop for your going-away outfit

Make-up and appearance
- Make an appointment to see your hairdresser to discuss your hairstyle and headdress (if having one)
- Make an appointment for a make-up lesson

Going away
- If you are going abroad for your honeymoon, ensure that you have a valid passport
- Arrange vaccinations

Invitations
- Begin to write out the invitations

Presents
- Set up a wedding list at a good department store that has a Bride's Department

Other
- See the doctor regarding family planning, if required

Invitations
● With your mother, send out the invitations

Presents
● Supply a wedding list to anyone who wants it
● Write thank-you letters as presents are received

Music
● Make sure of arrangements concerning musicians, bell-ringers, etc.

Reception
● With your parents, check that all bookings have been made; final confirmation of menu; order the drinks and hire glasses (if necessary)

Floral decorations
● Order flowers from the florist

Clothing
● Attend bridesmaids' clothes fittings; shop for accessories; ensure the groom has made arrangements for his wedding clothes

Bridesmaids
● Select the gifts for the bridesmaids

Other
● With your parents, arrange accommodation for anyone who might need it

- Obtain quotations for insurance against cancellation of the wedding and loss of or damage to attire and presents
- Arrange insurance

Clothing
- Pay for your wedding and going away outfits, and for those of the bridesmaids
- Think about what clothes you want to take on your honeymoon

Make-up and appearance
- Make appointments with the hairdresser, beautician/manicurist for the day before or on the wedding day

Reception
- If the cake is home-made, deliver it to the decorator to be professionally iced

Floral decorations
- Plan the arrangement of the flowers at church and reception if you or members of your family are responsible for them

Invitations
- With your parents, make sure that you have all the replies to the invitations – follow up any that have not been received

Other
- Buy the groom's wedding present

- Notify the bank, doctor, etc. if you plan to adopt the groom's surname
- Organize hen night for the week before the wedding (but *not* the night before)

Less than a month in advance

2
Weeks

Reception
- Advise the caterer and reception venue of the final number of guests
- Consult caterers regarding menu and finalize choice
- Sketch a seating plan
- Buy and start preparing food for a reception at home or in hired hall

Floral decorations
- Contact the florist to finalize/confirm the collection/delivery times for the flowers

Clothing
- Arrange for a final fitting, with your chief bridesmaid and (adult) bridesmaids, of all wedding clothes including underwear and shoes
- Ensure that your going away outfit is ready

Make-up and appearance
- Purchase and try out make-up for the day. Keep it all in one place
- If having a shorter hairstyle, get your hair done now

Reception
- Check on all the arrangements

Clothing
- Take delivery of wedding clothes
- Wear in wedding shoes

Stationery
- Collect any still outstanding

Floral decorations
- Confirm final plans concerning flowers and their arrangement

Other
- Make sure that the menfolk have organized their clothing and are writing their speeches
- Start packing for honeymoon
- Enjoy the hen night

Reception
- Decorate the hall, marquee, etc.
- See that the cake and table stationery are delivered to the reception venue or the hosts' home

Floral decorations
- If doing the flowers yourself, soak and prepare them

Clothing
- Iron (if necessary) and lay out wedding outfit

Make-up and appearance
- Go to the hairdresser and manicurist, unless you have appointments with them on the day

- Put some cosmetics and a hairbrush/comb in a small bag for last minute retouches before the ceremony, and before leaving the reception
- Have an early night

The day

Marriage ceremony
- Ensure that the best man has collected the order of service sheets and the buttonholes

Floral decorations
- Take delivery of the flowers
- Help to do the floral decorations in the church (if doing it yourself) and at the reception venue

Going away
- Ensure that the honeymoon clothes and baggage are taken to reception

Make-up and appearance
- Go to the hairdresser/manicurist/ beautician, or ask them to visit you at home, if you did not have an appointment the day before

See also 'Bride and groom's countdown chart', pp. 27–31

13. The groom

Role and responsibilities
Before the day

- Books the place of marriage and pays the fees
- Looks after the legal aspects of the wedding
- Chooses the best man and the ushers
- Organizes the honeymoon
- With the best man, makes arrangements for their wedding clothes
- With the bride, shops for the wedding ring(s)
- Pays for the flowers
- Buys presents for bridesmaids
- Prepares his speech
- Attends wedding rehearsal

On the day: before the ceremony

- Checks that everything is in order
- Meets the best man and the ushers
- Arrives at church 20–30 minutes early
- Checks entry in the register
- In the register office, meets with the registrar to exchange papers

On the day: the ceremony

- Waits for the bride
- Signs the register
- With the bride, heads the recessional

On the day: at the reception

- Takes part in receiving the guests
- Delivers his speech
- With the bride, leaves for the honeymoon

Before the day

BOOKING THE PLACE OF MARRIAGE
Conventionally, the groom has the task of booking the
church or register office. He also makes appointments
to see the clergyman or superintendent registrar.

PAYING THE FEES
He is responsible for all marriage and church fees,
such as for the choir, bells and floral decorations (see
'Register Office Weddings', pp. 81 and 86, and
'Church weddings', pp. 94-5 and 105).

LEGAL RESPONSIBILITIES
He must also supply the information necessary for the
marriage application to be accepted. With a register
office wedding, it is the groom's responsibility to
collect the certificate of marriage, or the
superintendent registrar's licence, at the appointed
time, to pay the appropriate fee, and to make sure he
presents whichever one he has to the registrar on the
day of the wedding (see 'Marriage and the law',
pp. 40–3). The groom is also responsible for ensuring
that documents, such as certificates and licences, that
may be required for a religious ceremony have been
obtained (see pp. 35–43). If the marriage is to take
place in an Anglican church, authorized by banns, and
he comes from a different parish, the groom must
coordinate the readings of the banns in both churches
(see 'Marriage and the law', pp. 34–5).

CHOOSING THE ATTENDANTS
Once he has dealt with his financial and legal

responsibilites, the groom chooses his best man (see
'The best man', pp. 258-9), and his ushers (see 'The
ushers', p. 287), although the latter are not necessary
for a register office as the number of guests may be
restricted owing to the size of the marriage rooms.

ORGANIZING THE HONEYMOON

By far the largest item of expenditure on the groom's
agenda is the honeymoon. At one time, tradition held
that the groom should pleasantly surprise his bride with
their honeymoon destination, as they prepared to depart
from the reception. Nowadays, the tendency is to make
a joint decision. However, the groom still pays for the
trip and makes all the arrangements including travel,
accommodation, immunization (if the location is
tropical), insurance and currency. The groom is also
responsible for the safe-keeping of all documents until
the morning of the wedding, when he entrusts them to
his best man.

HIRING THE WEDDING CLOTHES

If the couple has decided on a formal wedding with the
men wearing morning suits or other appropriate dress
(such as kilts), then the groom should arrange with his
best man to hire outfits (see 'The best man', pp.
262–3), for themselves and the ushers, and have them
delivered on time. (The best man is responsible for their
return after the wedding.) The groom also pays for the
hire of all the suits: he does not have to buy outfits for
his best man or for his ushers. If, however, the wedding
is not so formal as to require morning suits, the groom
should consider buying a lounge or dinner suit and his
attendants should wear something similar.

SHOPPING FOR THE WEDDING RING(S)

One of the groom's more pleasurable duties is to escort his bride to choose her wedding ring – his, too, if their plan is to exchange rings. Once the choice has been made, the groom is responsible for collecting and paying for the rings, and for their safe-keeping until the morning of the wedding. He then passes the rings to the best man, who keeps them until the appropriate point in the ceremony.

PAYING FOR THE FLOWERS

The groom traditionally pays for the bride's bouquet, according to *Debrett's Book of Etiquette*. Sometimes he pays for all the flowers – church decorations, bridesmaids' posies, both mothers' corsages and the guests' buttonholes. But very often, the bride's father will add this expense to his own bill. Payment for the flowers really depends on individual arrangements.

GIFTS FOR THE BRIDE AND ATTENDANTS

It is customary for the bride and groom to give each other presents, and to present gifts to their attendants as a token of their thanks and appreciation – it is usual for the groom to pay for these.

Bridesmaids

It is a convention that, at the reception, the groom presents the bridesmaids with gifts after his speech. The bride and the groom should select the gifts together – though, traditionally, it is the groom who pays for them.

PREPARING THE SPEECH

By far the most arduous task facing the groom is the speech he must make to the wedding party after the meal at the reception (see 'Toasts and speeches', pp. 300-1). Whether or not he feels he can speak in public, he is the one speechmaker who cannot pass the burden on to someone else. The guests will expect him to respond to the toast proposed by the bride's father (the first to speak), to say a few words himself, and to propose a toast to the bridesmaids.

Content

The speech need not be an ordeal, however, if the groom prepares well and practises. He should base what he is going to say on thanking various people (see 'Toasts and speeches', p. 301). He could relieve the possible monotony of these thanks by introducing amusing anecdotes, such as how he met his bride, problems they had during the wedding preparations, or how he had to persuade his best man to stand by him. Finally, he proposes a toast to the bridesmaids, to which the best man responds on their behalf.

Length and practice

The speech should not take more than five minutes, and the groom can practise by timing himself delivering the speech in a slow, distinct tone. Looking at himself in the mirror will also help him to control any nervous habits or twitches. He may find it helpful to have short notes written on prompt cards, and to memorize the opening words and short phrases linking the subjects of the speech (see pp. 298-9).

ATTENDING THE WEDDING REHEARSAL

His last duty before the wedding day is to attend the wedding rehearsal, if the ceremony is to take place in church. He joins the bride, best man and chief bridesmaid in going through the order of service with the clergyman in order to make sure each knows what to do on the day.

CARS FOR THE WEDDING PARTY
If he and/or his family have opted to pay for the wedding cars, then the groom should ask the best man to take responsibility for making the arrangements (see 'The best man', pp. 261-2).

On the day

BEFORE THE CEREMONY
Checking that everything is in order
On the morning of the wedding, the groom has to collect his suit (if he is hiring his outfit) and get ready. Before he leaves the house, he should check he has the rings, the certificate of marriage or the superintendent registrar's licence (if the wedding is taking place in a register office), the marriage schedule (in Scotland), his speech, the bridesmaids' presents, telemessages and the honeymoon documents.

Meeting with the attendants beforehand
He should arrange to meet the best man and ushers at least an hour before the time of the wedding. This gives them all a final opportunity to rehearse their duties at the ceremony, and he can hand over the rings, presents and documents to the best man. The ushers go on to the church to receive the guests, but the groom and best man need not arrive until 20–30 minutes before the ceremony. If the ceremony is at a church, the groom will be required by the clergyman to check the entry in the register before the wedding.

THE CEREMONY
Waiting for the bride
For a church ceremony, the groom and best man sit in
the first pew on the right side of the aisle facing the
altar, in front of his family and friends. He awaits the
bride and stands to receive her when he hears the
wedding march being played. (This is a signal for all
the congregation that she has entered the church.) In a
register office, he should arrive before the bride and,
after a short consultation with the registrar when papers
are exchanged (see 'Register office weddings',
pp. 83-6), he waits for the bride at the registrar's table,
again sitting on the right.
The ring
At both religious and civil ceremonies, the groom
stands on the bride's right as the clergyman or registrar
conducts the ceremony. At the appointed time, the best
man places the rings on the prayer book offered by the
minister (church wedding) or gives them to the groom
(register office wedding). The groom places the ring on
the third finger of his bride's left hand as directed by
the clergyman, at which point they are married. In a
civil ceremony, the ring is not strictly necessary, and so
the groom puts it on his bride's finger after the registrar
has married them.
Signing the register
If the marriage takes place in church, the bride and
groom head the procession into the vestry to sign the
marriage register (see 'Church weddings', p. 101).
Leaving the church
After the signing of the register, the bridal party leaves
the vestry and walks down the aisle (the recessional;

see pp. 101-3) and out of the church for the photos (see 'Arranging the photography', pp. 181-2).

At the register office

At a register office, the bride and groom and two witnesses sign the register at the registrar's table. They may then leave the room in the same order of procession as for the church ceremony, but this is not strictly necessary.

AT THE RECEPTION

Receiving the guests

The groom usually travels to the reception with his bride in the car which brought her and her father to the church. At the reception hall, he joins the receiving line and greets his guests after the bride's parents, his parents and the bride.

Position at the top table

The groom takes his place at the centre right of the top table, between his bride on his left and her mother on his right (see 'Arranging the reception', p. 132).

Delivering the speech and leading the dancing

After the meal, when the bride's father has made his speech and proposed a toast to the newlyweds, the groom rises and speaks to his guests, finishing with a toast to the bridesmaids. He then gives each of the latter a personal present as a thank-you for their services to his new wife. After the best man has made the final speech and read the greetings and messages, the groom takes the floor with his bride, if there is dancing.

Leaving for the honeymoon

At an appointed time, perhaps to fit in with travel plans, the groom and his bride change into their going-away outfits and prepare to leave the reception. The best man gives the groom any travel documents he has been keeping for him, and the newlyweds depart for their honeymoon.

Groom's checklist
Before the day

What you pay for
- Clergyman's fee (for a church wedding)
- Church services – organist, choir, bells, flowers
- Registrar's fee and the fee for the certificate of marriage or superintendent registrar's licence (for a register office wedding)
- Wedding ring or rings
- Hire of morning suits for yourself, the best man and ushers (for a formal wedding); buy your own suit, if preferred
- Bride's bouquet (possibly other flowers too, depending on individual arrangements)
- Honeymoon (traditionally)

What you are responsible for organizing
- Marriage ceremony with the clergyman or superintendent registrar
- Purchase of the wedding ring or rings
- Hire of your own morning suit (if applicable)
- Preparing your speech
- Gifts for the bridesmaids
- Honeymoon

The groom's countdown chart follows overleaf.

On the day

- Arrange to meet the best man before the ceremony and entrust him with honeymoon documents and the ring
- Arrive at the church or register office with the best man at least 20–30 minutes before the ceremony
- Check the entry in the marriage register
- Take your place at the front of the right side of the church or marriage room
- Rise to meet the bride as she walks up the aisle or into the room
- Place the ring on the third finger of her left hand as directed by the clergyman or registrar
- Sign the marriage register
- Greet the guests in the receiving line at the reception
- Respond to the bride's father's toast; make the speech and propose a toast to the bridesmaids, giving them personal presents as tokens of thanks
- Lead the dancing with the bride
- Retrieve the honeymoon documents from the best man, change into your going-away clothes and leave the reception with the bride

Groom's countdown chart

**Months
in advance**

6
Months

Marriage ceremony and legalities
- Find out the details about getting an Archbishop of Canterbury's special licence or Registrar General's licence, if needed

Best man and ushers
- Choose the best man

Going away
- Book the honeymoon

4
Months

Clothing
- If the dress is to be formal, you, the best man and the other leading men should hire morning suits; if not, begin to look around for and to buy new suits, if required

3
Months

Marriage ceremony and legalities
- Book the register office, if you are having a civil ceremony
- Give notice to the superintendent registrar, if your wedding is not Church of England

Going away
- Ensure that you and your bride each possess a valid passport, if you are honeymooning abroad
- Arrange vaccinations, if required

Cars
- Ask the best man to organize cars for the wedding party, and to check that they are insured
- With the bride, select and pay for the wedding rings

Clothing
- Buy your going-away clothes
- Think about your honeymoon clothes

Going away
- Make final arrangements for the honeymoon

Marriage ceremony and legalities
- If a civil ceremony, obtain the certificate and the licence (or marriage schedule) from the registrar
- Buy the bride's wedding present and gifts for attendants

Cars
- If hiring cars, check that they have been booked for the wedding day

Other
- Pay for the bridesmaids' gifts

- Organize stag night for the week before the wedding (but *not* the night before)

**Less than
a month
in advance**

Going away
● Order traveller's cheques and foreign
  currency for the honeymoon

Cars
● Finalize transport arrangements
Clothing
● Confirm arrangements for your own,
  the best man's and the ushers' clothes
Going away
● Give the best man the honeymoon
  tickets, etc.
Other
● Prepare your speech
● Enjoy the stag night

Cars
● Clean and decorate borrowed cars
● Ensure that borrowed cars are filled
  with petrol
Clothing
● Press and lay out wedding outfit
Going away
● Pack your honeymoon suitcase

Other
- Visit the barber/ hairdresser unless you intend to on the day
- Have an early night

Cars
- Check arrival time of the wedding cars

Other
- Visit the barber/hairdresser, if you have not already done so

See also 'Bride and groom's countdown chart', pp. 27-31

14. The bride's mother

Role and responsibilities
Before the day

- Arranges the reception
- Compiles the guest list and sends the invitations
- Draws up a seating plan
- Notifies the local or national press (if desired) of the marriage
- Helps to choose the bride's and bridesmaids' dresses
- Organizes the flowers
- Hires the wedding cars
- Helps to book the photographer
- Chooses her outfit
- Arranges accommodation for the guests

On the day: before the ceremony

- Ensures the best man has collected the service sheets and buttonholes
- Helps to dress the bride
- Supervises the bridesmaids

On the day: the ceremony

- Is present at the signing of the register
- Participates in the recessional

On the day: at the reception

- Receives the guests
- Possibly clears up

The responsibilities, given here are those that traditionally belong to the bride's mother. Often, however, her role overlaps with that of her daughter. These roles may also be entirely assumed by the bride or the bridal couple, or shared with the bride's mother.

ORGANIZING EVERYTHING

If the bride's parents are footing the bill for the entire affair, then the bride's mother is likely to have the final say in the organization of the reception, the printing of the wedding stationery, the purchase or hire of the bride's and bridesmaids' outfits and her own, the choice of flowers and photographer, and any other costs dependent on the budget.

Using hired professionals

If she decides to hire professionals to fulfil most of these tasks, then they will take much of the burden from her and guide her decision as to the best available service for the price affordable. All she need do is make contact with the relevant firms in good time to ensure they can provide their services on the date of the wedding, and keep a constant watch on how matters are proceeding (see 'Arranging the reception', pp. 106-143).

Before the day

ARRANGING THE RECEPTION
At home

For a small wedding, the bride's mother may choose to hold the reception in her own home and do the catering herself. If this is the case, then much of the physical work falls to her, although relatives, friends and neighbours usually offer to help share the load. But she must make the decision on what food and drink to have, then she must buy it, prepare the food and organize seating, china, cutlery and glasses for the day.

Hiring caterers and a marquee

The family may opt to hire caterers, and perhaps have a marquee on the lawn. In these cases, the bride's mother needs to organize and coordinate the different services so that things go smoothly on the day.

Choosing the menu

When the style of reception has been decided – whether based on cost or preference – the bride's mother should arrange to see menus from which she can choose. Her decision should be based on what most people are likely to eat, although this should not stop her being adventurous, particularly if the meal is a buffet (see 'Arranging the reception', pp. 110-5, for food ideas.)

Other services and facilities

The bride's mother should also see about other services provided by the caterers or venue, such as cloakrooms and separate rooms in which the couple change and in which presents may be displayed (see p. 107).

Organizing the wedding cake

One of the key arrangements to make for any reception is the ordering or making of the wedding cake. The bride will probably have expressed a preference regarding the style and colour of cake she would like. Her mother, therefore, need only carry out her wishes by organizing its production and delivery to the reception venue on the eve of the wedding (see pp. 122-8.).

COMPILING THE GUEST LIST

The bride's guest list

The bride's mother has the extremely diplomatic task of finalizing the guest list. She must remember that, even

if she and her husband are paying for the event, she
should not allocate the lion's share of the guest list to
her own side (see 'Wedding invitations', pp. 144-6).

The groom's guest list

She should request a provisional list from the groom's
mother, indicating the approximate numbers. This
should include how many may attend the service – if it
is to be held in a small church or a register office where
numbers will be restricted, for example.

Pruning both lists (if necessary)

She may have to refuse to accommodate all the groom's
guests, if his parents provide a list of names outside the
set limits. How she does this may tax her powers of
diplomacy. Possibly the best solution is to arrange an
informal meeting with the groom's mother so they can
go through their lists together. This will demonstrate
clearly any need to restrict numbers. Very often, the
groom's mother will be happy to prune the list, thus
making the task less challenging.

INVITATIONS

Once the guest list is finalized, the bride's mother
writes and posts the invitations, which have been
worded to show that she and her husband are the hosts.
Even if they are not (the bride and groom may be
funding their wedding themselves, or the couple have
compiled the list themselves), convention dictates that
the invitations come from the bride's parents (see
'Wedding invitations', p. 147).

Choosing the style of invitation

The bride's mother should consult her daughter as to
whether she prefers standard invitation cards, or a

custom-printed design, and then should order them in
good time for them to be sent out. The invitations
should be sent in good time to ensure most guests will
have the day free. About two to three months should be
adequate (see 'Wedding invitations', pp. 144-165).

Other stationery

While ordering the invitations, other stationery (see
'Arranging the reception', p. 128), such as name cards,
napkins and order of service sheets, can be organized so
that all the printing is taken care of at one time.

SEATING PLAN

Once the bride's mother has received the replies from
the guests, she is able to compile a final list and set
about drawing up a seating plan, if the reception is a
formal meal or sit-down buffet. The top table presents
no problem, but who sits with whom among the guests,
and with what precedence, will often develop into a
complicated juggling act as the bride's mother strives to
seat everyone in a pleasing position.

The likes and dislikes of the guests

She must take into account likes and dislikes among
members of her family, and also that of the groom. His
mother will be invaluable here in advising which
relatives to avoid placing together and which to seat in
a prominent position as befits their station in the family.

Deciding whether to integrate the families

It used to be the convention that members of the same
family were seated together, thus creating 'sides'.
However, some families opt to intermingle families and
friends in the hope of generating a more integrated
atmosphere. This may not work, however, if both sides

are not particularly gregarious – a universal silence may result. The bride's mother must decide. If this proves difficult, she should play safe and keep each family together. Very often, they will begin to mingle anyway after the meal, when everyone is more relaxed.

PRESS ANNOUNCEMENTS

As well as sending invitations, the bride's mother may wish to notify the local or national press of her daughter's forthcoming marriage, and so should contact the listings department at the relevant newspaper office. If a picture of the wedding is required for a report after the day, the bride's mother should arrange for the photographer to produce a print that is slightly more blue than normal (to fit printing requirements) which she can send to the newspaper office as soon as possible after the wedding. If the paper cannot send its own reporter, often a standard form is sent out on which details of names, families, backgrounds, dress and flowers can be recorded and sent to the office for publication.

THE BRIDE'S AND BRIDESMAIDS' DRESSES
Cost

Cost may dictate the number of bridesmaids, pages and flowergirls her daughter may have, but the wise mother will try not to curb the bride's choice of dress on grounds of cost. Conversely, her daughter should be aware from the outset what the budget is likely to be.

Helping to choose the bride's dress

Many mothers regard helping their daughter choose her wedding dress as one of the most personal moments they will ever share. She must also recognize, however, that there may be marked differences in fashion preferences, and she should not insist on her own choice because she is paying for it (*if* she is paying for it). Rather, she should guide her daughter and then leave her to make the final decision on the style of both her own and her bridesmaids' dresses.

Buy, hire or make?

One decision the bride and her mother may have to make is whether the dress should be bought, hired or made (see 'The bride', pp. 201-6). Cost may force the decision. Whichever is chosen, the bride's mother should take charge of the arrangements, but consult her daughter at every step.

ORGANIZING THE FLOWERS
Cost

Though her daughter might dream of a church overflowing with blooms as she walks up the aisle with a bouquet which trails to the floor, the bride's mother must exercise all her tact to induce a choice of flowers that fits the budget, even if it is the groom who is paying for these.

Ordering the flowers

Once the decisions have been made, the bride's mother will choose the florist and place the order in good time for delivery either the day before or on the morning of the wedding (see 'Ordering the flowers', pp. 166-76).

HIRING THE WEDDING CARS

Most brides have at least one hired car to take them and their fathers to the place of marriage. This may be something special, such as a vintage Rolls-Royce or a carriage and four, so the bride's mother needs to investigate all possibilities according to her daughter's wishes – within the budget, of course.

Sharing the responsibility

If both the bride's and the groom's families have decided to share the costs of the wedding, very often the groom's family will pay for the cars, and the best man will make the arrangements (see 'The groom', p. 227, and 'The best man', pp. 261-2). If, however, the bride's parents are shouldering entirely the financial responsibility, then it is down to the bride's mother (or, indeed, her father) to organize the wedding cars.

Priority for hired cars

The provision of other cars is usually a matter of cost. Conventionally, the bridesmaids ride in a second car, followed by the bride's mother, and any other members of the bride's immediate family, in another. There is no reason why all the family cannot be accommodated in a convoy of ceremonial cars if the budget allows.

Hiring cars from more than one firm

The bride's mother need not hire all the cars from one firm. However, she must coordinate their times of arrival, and make sure all the cars have adequate insurance for the day.

BOOKING THE PHOTOGRAPHER

Next to the bridal couple themselves, the bride's mother is probably the person who most wants to see the wedding beautifully recorded. Therefore, she is in the best position to thwart keen amateur photographers in the family from volunteering themselves as official photographers. She should help her daughter and the groom to select a suitable professional photographer and make all the arrangements for his attendance at the wedding and the reception (see 'Arranging the photography', pp. 177-83).

CHOOSING AN OUTFIT

Up until now, the bride's mother has occupied herself with making sure everything goes to plan for her daughter. But of importance, too, is how she will look herself on the day. It is one time when the bride's mother may feel she deserves a designer dress to brighten the occasion, or to complement the formal attire of the men.

Having time to make the right choice

The bride's mother should allow enough time in her hectic schedule for browsing through the shops in order to find the right outfit, leaving enough time also to have any alterations made if needed.

Selecting a style to suit the season

Conventionally, the bride's mother should dress for the season – a lightweight dress, or suit, and light hat for a summer wedding; a more formal suit, or coat-and-dress, and warmer hat for the cooler weather of spring, autumn or winter. She usually wears gloves, and therefore has to think of co-ordinating all elements to produce a pleasing effect.

Choosing a suitable colour

She may take her cue on colour from those chosen for the bride's bouquet, or decide to be completely different to create a contrast. However, she should take care not to outshine her daughter or choose something out of keeping with the tenor of the occasion.

Avoiding embarrassment on the day

Always a possibility, when the bride's mother chooses
an outfit, is that she might arrive at the wedding in
clothes identical to those of the groom's mother. But
unless they are of similar age and have similar tastes,
and the town they live in boasts only one or two
outfitters, this is unlikely to happen. However, if the
two mothers have become acquainted, they could each
give an indication of the colour and style of clothes
they are likely to choose.

ARRANGING ACCOMMODATION

The bride's mother is the hostess for the wedding day,
and therefore may need to take on the responsibility of
arranging accommodation for family or friends who are
travelling from out of town. This may be either in her
own home or with relatives or friends, or in nearby
hotels. She should offer to find out the times of buses
and trains for people travelling by public transport and,
if possible, arrange for them to be collected from the
station. She will probably invite her own guests to call
into her house before the ceremony for some
refreshment, especially if some are staying in hotels or
travelling long distances on the day.

On the day

Most of the bride's mother's work has already been
done and so, besides checking, from early morning and
throughout the day, that everything is going according
to plan, she can enjoy the occasion of her daughter's
wedding.

BEFORE THE CEREMONY

Early in the day, the bride's mother should make sure
that the best man has collected the buttonholes, service
sheets and any telemessages that may have arrived.

Dressing the bride and supervising the bridesmaids
Her most important preparatory role (with the chief
bridesmaid) is to help her daughter dress for the
ceremony, to arrange for last-minute visits from the
hairdresser or dressmaker if necessary, and to help the
bride into her dress and veil. If the bride has any last-
minute nerves, then the bride's mother can also be of
invaluable help in calming her. The bride's mother
should then take time to dress, and make sure the
bridesmaids are ready when the cars arrive. She travels
to the church or register office in advance of the bride,
and is usually the last person to be seated.

THE CEREMONY

Signing of the register and the recessional
In a church ceremony, the bride's mother is escorted to
her place, in the front pew on the left-hand side of the
aisle, by the chief usher. She takes no part in the
marriage until the signing of the register, when she
follows the best man and chief bridesmaid, in the
company of the groom's father, into the vestry. She
does not sign the register unless she is one of the
witnesses. On leaving the vestry, she walks with the
groom's father down the aisle, in front of her husband
and the groom's mother, and then outside for
photographs.

AT THE RECEPTION

The bride's mother travels to the reception with her

husband in the third car in the procession, or with the groom's father, depending on preference. Upon arrival, she organizes the receiving line to greet the guests, and she will be the first to welcome them. Thereafter, she takes her place at the top table, either beside her husband or next to the groom's father, whichever has been arranged. As hostess, she should circulate among the guests after the formalities, making the acquaintance of those she does not know and generally helping everyone to enjoy the occasion.

Clearing up
Hired premises and caterers
Once the celebrations have come to an end, the bride's mother should settle any outstanding arrangements, with regard to the reception venue – safe-keeping of the presents overnight, for example – and with the caterers regarding the disposal of the remainder of the cake: it is usually packed so she can take it home.

Self-catering celebrations
If she has organized the catering herself, perhaps in a hired hall, then the bride's mother should supervise the clearing up, setting members of the family various tasks to help her. She should be the last to leave the hired hall, making sure that everything has been cleared away, the lights are out and that the door is locked.

Bride's mother's checklist
Before the day

- Arrange the reception/catering; choose menu
- If catering at home or in a hired hall, decide on the food to be offered and arrange for its purchase and preparation

- Organize the wedding cake
- Compile the guest list with the aid of the groom's mother
- Order the invitations (and any other wedding stationery) and send them out
- Draw up a seating plan according to the replies to the invitations, consulting the groom's family regarding positioning guests
- Help the bride choose her outfit and that of the bridesmaids
- Organize making or hiring of wedding dress
- Arrange the flowers and church decorations
- Hire the wedding cars (unless the best man is doing so on behalf of the groom)
- Book the photographer
- Choose your own outfit
- Make last-minute checks that all is going to plan

On the day

- Ensure all deliveries and arrangements are going to plan
- Help the bride to dress (can be delegated to the chief bridesmaid)
- Supervise the bridesmaids
- Take your seat in the place of marriage just before the bride enters
- Join the bridal procession with the groom's father to enter the vestry for the signing of the register
- Participate in the recessional, again with the groom's father
- Greet the guests as first person in the receiving line
- Attend to any clearing up or final arrangements at the end of the celebrations

15. The bride's father

Role and responsibilities

Before the day

- Is responsible for paying for the celebrations
- Prepares a speech for the reception
- Hires/buys a wedding suit

On the day: before the ceremony

- Ensures wedding transport arrives in good time
- Ensures everyone sets off for the place of marriage in time
- Escorts the bride to the place of marriage

On the day: the ceremony

- Escorts the bride up the aisle
- Gives the bride away
- Present at the signing of the register

On the day: at the reception

- Receives the guests
- Delivers the speech

The roles set out in this chapter are those that traditionally belong to the bride's father. But, of course, any or all of his responsibilities may be undertaken by the bridal couple themselves or other members of the bride's family or friends. On the other hand, the bride's father may choose to be far more involved in making the arrangements with his wife and/or daughter than he is conventionally required or expected to be.

Before the day

THE BUDGET
Sharing the costs

As soon as the wedding date is set, the bride's father should arrange a meeting between himself, his wife and his future son-in-law's parents to decide on who is going to finance the venture. Very often, the couples will already be acquainted, and shared responsibility for the costs may already be a foregone conclusion, but the bride's father should not expect the groom's parents to share the bill, nor should he be offended if they do not offer.

Who pays for what

However, most parents are aware of the colossal cost of even the most modest wedding and will gladly offer as much financial support as they can, so that their son and their future daughter-in-law might have the wedding they want. If sharing the costs is agreed, a list of who will pay for what should be drawn up to avoid confusion later on.

Going it alone

If the bride's father prefers to fund his daughter's wedding on his own, then he should set his budget as early on as possible. He should advise his daughter and the groom whether or not this will stretch to all the trimmings they envisage for their big day. If they set their sights too high, and incur expenses far beyond his means, the bride's father will only have the uncomfortable choice of either telling them to cancel what he cannot afford, or to put himself in debt. Either of these eventualities will spoil the occasion for him.

Planning ahead

Many fathers, however, will have planned for the occasion years before, possibly when their daughter was born. They may have saved for this specifically, or taken out an endowment insurance policy to mature when their daughter reached her early twenties.

PREPARING THE SPEECH

Apart from traditionally providing the means for the wedding to take place, the bride's father plays no further role, except for advising where necessary, until the day of the wedding. Many fathers will choose, though, to share most of the responsibilities for arranging the reception, car hire and so on, with the bride's mother. Besides giving his daughter away, the bride's father's most visible role in this is the speech he traditionally makes at the wedding reception, where he is the first to speak.

Finding a stand-in

If he feels unable to perform this task (possibly he is a shy man and is afraid of letting his daughter down), then he should not agonize over his discomfort and spoil the day for himself, but should immediately tell his daughter of his decision to pass on this responsibility – perhaps to a more flamboyant brother, a perfectly acceptable substitute as uncle of the bride. The other man concerned should be approached as early as possible, so he may prepare his speech.

Where the stand-in sits

There is no need for the uncle, or whoever is called upon to make the opening speech, to take the father's place at the top table. He can rise and speak from the

body of the guests at the appropriate time, which will
be signalled to him by the best man.

Practising the speech

Most men, however, will do their best to overcome
feelings of nervousness and inadequacy for the sake of
a daughter, and will go a long way to ensure success
with thorough preparation and practice.

Content

The bride's father should decide on what the main
points of his speech will be (see 'Toasts and speeches',
pp. 299-300).

Style

He need not feel inadequate if he cannot make his
speech uproariously funny – the bridal couple and the
guests will appreciate his sincerity, however simply
demonstrated. In fact, it is probably better if he leaves
most of the jokes to the best man: he is an authority
figure during the proceedings and should fulfil this role.

WEDDING SUIT

Buying a suit

Once he has prepared his speech, the bride's father has
the pleasurable task of deciding on his wedding attire.
Possibly this is the one occasion when he can justify the
expense of a new suit. If so, he should choose a formal,
neutral colour – dark grey or navy blue. A white, or
predominantly white, shirt and sober tie will complete
the formal effect.

Hiring a suit

The decision of what to wear, however, may have
already been taken for him if the bride and groom have
decided that morning suits (or other appropriate formal

dress, such as kilts) will be worn by the leading men (groom, best man, ushers, bride's father, groom's father). Unless he already has a suit of his own, the bride's father should consult with the groom about hiring similar outfits, so that they achieve a coordinated effect on the day. The groom may even order the suit for him, and the bride's father may accompany the others to fittings, but he should pay his own costs. If he decides to organize his own hired suit, he should do so well in advance so that it will definitely be ready for the wedding.

On the day

BEFORE THE CEREMONY
Ensuring everyone sets off in time
The role of the bride's father is central to the early proceedings of the wedding day. His most important task begins as the bride prepares to leave her home for the church or register office. He must make sure the cars arrive in good time to take the bridesmaids, his wife and any other members of the family, and himself and the bride to where the ceremony will take place. He helps his daughter into the bridal car, making sure her dress is not crushed.

THE CEREMONY
Escorting and giving away the bride
At the church, or register office, the bridesmaids will assist in straightening the bride's dress and veil. The bride's father greets the clergyman – who often welcomes the wedding party at the door – or the registrar. He then accompanies the bride inside,

walking up the aisle or to the front of the marriage room on her left. He remains with her until that part of the ceremony where the minister asks: 'Who gives this woman?' The bride's father may reply: 'I do' (although this is not compulsory), guide his daughter to the groom's side and then retire a few paces. This symbolizes her departure from his family, his protection and his authority.

Signing the register

After the marriage rites have been performed, during a church ceremony, the bride's father, escorting the groom's mother, follows his wife and the groom's father (preceded by the bridal couple), and the chief bridesmaid and the best man into the vestry for the signing of the marriage register. He does not normally add his signature to the register unless he is one of the witnesses. He occupies the same position in the recession down the aisle and out of the church for the photographs.

Leaving for the reception

The bride's father does not ride with his daughter to the reception, but takes his place with his wife in the third bridal car, following the second car taking the best man and bridesmaids. Alternatively, he may accompany the groom's mother in the fourth car, while the groom's father rides with his wife in the third car.

AT THE RECEPTION
Receiving the guests

Upon arriving at the reception rooms, he joins the welcoming line and is second to greet the guests, after his wife.

Position at the top table

He then takes his place at his daughter's left side at the top table for the meal (see 'Arranging the reception', p. 132).

Delivering the speech

The best man will signal the appropriate time for him to rise and deliver his carefully prepared speech. After he has proposed a toast to the happy couple, he may relax and enjoy the rest of the celebrations. It only remains for him, as host, to circulate amongst the guests and help them enjoy the occasion.

Bride's father's checklist

Before the day

- Decide on how much you can afford to spend on your daughter's wedding (if you alone are financing it)
- Redeem any policies maturing for such an occasion, or arrange any necessary loan to meet the costs
- If sharing the costs with the groom's parents, arrange a meeting to decide who will pay for what
- Write and prepare speech well in advance
- Practise speech until confident of a successful delivery
- Choose and buy wedding ensemble. If morning dress is to be worn, arrange hire of the suit

On the day

- Ensure the bridal cars arrive on time
- Make sure the bride is ready to leave on time
- Accompany the bride to the church or register office

- Walk with her up the aisle or to the front of the marriage room
- Give her away at the appropriate moment in the ceremony
- Join the procession to the vestry for the signing of the register
- Bring up the rear with the groom's mother in the recessional
- Greet the guests in the receiving line at the reception
- Give the first speech after the meal
- Propose the first toast to the newlyweds

16. The best man

Role and responsibilities
Before the day

- Confirms the arrangements concerning the place of marriage: date, time, number of people, etc.
- Pays the clergyman/registrar on behalf of the groom
- Takes responsibility for transport and parking arrangements
- Hires clothes for himself, the groom and the ushers
- Writes the speech
- Arranges the stag night
- Attends the wedding rehearsal

On the day: before the ceremony

- Collects the service sheets and buttonholes from the bride's mother
- Makes sure he has the bride's wedding ring
- Ensures that the groom gets to the place of marriage on time

On the day: at the church

- Organizes the ushers
- Organizes the positions of the participants in the procession to the vestry and the recessional
- Signs the register
- Directs and times the photographer
- Informs the guests of transport arrangements to the reception

On the day: at the reception

- Introduces the speeches at the reception
- Reads out the telemessages

- Proposes a toast and invites the bridal couple to cut the cake
- Supervises the decoration of the groom's car
- Ensures a smooth getaway for the bridal couple
- Brings the celebrations to a close

On the wedding day itself, the best man is at his most visible when he hands the ring to the groom during the marriage service and makes his speech at the reception. However, there is a great deal of behind-the-scenes work for him to do both before and on the day.

The groom's responsibility: before the day

CHOOSING THE BEST MAN

The groom needs to be extremely careful in his selection of his best man. Traditionally, the role is offered to the groom's closest, unmarried, adult male relative or friend. If this person is responsible and has a flair for organization, so much the better. If not, the groom will have to think again, as it is neither fair on this person nor on himself and his bride to burden someone with responsibilities he cannot cope with. It is far better to explain tactfully why another choice has been made, and get any disappointment over with early on, than to risk wrecking the wedding day itself.

ACCEPTING/REFUSING THE ROLE

At the same time, the man invited to take on the role should think carefully before he accepts whether he feels confident he can discharge the duties with success.

The best man's role: before the day

While responsibility for most of the wedding arrangements fall to the bride and her family, the best man's duties are just as important.

MEETING THE BRIDE'S FAMILY

The best man's first duty is to meet the bride and her parents, together with the groom, to decide who will take which responsibilities. Apart from putting relationships on a friendly footing, this will avoid duplication of duties which either the bride's or groom's side can undertake.

HELPING WITH THE 'BUSINESS SIDE'

The best man organizes the groom and his ushers, but he can also be of immense value helping with the 'business side' of the arrangements. For example, once the bride and groom have chosen the church or register office where the ceremony is to take place, the best man can confirm the arrangements, such as the date, time, number of guests expected, and he can check the cost of the services provided. In the case of a church, these may include the marriage fee, organist, choir, bells and flowers.

THE PLACE OF MARRIAGE AND ITS STAFF

Traditionally, the groom pays the clergyman or the registrar, but usually the best man hands over the fees, preferably in advance. This avoids the rather inappropriate spectacle of money changing hands on the wedding day, when the best man has more important duties to attend to. A good time to do this would be at the wedding rehearsal (if the ceremony is in church) which takes place during the week before the marriage. Failing that, making payment about quarter of an hour before the ceremony is due to start is usual (see p. 105).

PARKING ARRANGEMENTS

One of the most important considerations at both the place of marriage and the reception venue is the provision of parking, particularly if either or both venues is in the centre of a busy town. Many of the invited guests may be travelling some distance. There is no point in risking a bad atmosphere as guests arrive on time but have to rush around looking for a parking space. If both the place of marriage and the reception venue have large car parks, then there is nothing further to do. If not, the best man should investigate nearby parking facilities and inform the bride's family, so they may write to the guests, possibly with a map, to let them know what is available.

ARRANGING TRANSPORT FOR GUESTS

Of course, it is very likely that many guests will not have transport – elderly aunts, for example. So, the best man should offer to arrange transport for them, by contacting members of both sides who have cars, and organize lifts to the church, to the reception and, most importantly, home. Many families will do this themselves as a matter of course; but if the best man checks that everyone is catered for, then last-minute panics and disappointments will be avoided.

CARS FOR THE WEDDING PARTY

The most important transport arrangements, however, are those for the bride and groom and the wedding party. Convention dictates that this reponsibility belongs to the bride's parents (scc 'The bride's mother', p. 242-3) as, traditionally, the bride's father pays all wedding expenses; but if the two families have agreed to share the ever-soaring costs, then it is likely the groom's side will offer to pay for the cars.

Helping to organize the car hire

If the groom's family are paying for the car hire, then the best man can help (see 'The groom', p. 227). First, he should check the number of cars required. There are usually at least two: for the bride and her father, and for the bride's mother and bridesmaids. There may be more, however, depending on how much the couple wants to spend. A reasonable calculation for the best man to make would be a car for each of the following: the bride and her father; the bridesmaids, the bride's mother and other close family, for example, grandparents; the groom and himself; the groom's parents and/or grandparents.

Obtaining quotations

Having checked these requirements with both families, the best man should obtain quotations from several reputable hire firms locally. He will need to give them the exact times and locations at which the cars will be required.

Financial requirements

The best man should handle the financial side, but this time paying only a deposit on behalf of the groom, leaving the full amount to be settled when the service has been successfully rendered. This could be by paying the principal driver on the day (which can be done discreetly, as the wedding party has usually gone into the reception at this stage) or by paying the hire firm a few days later. The best man should find out beforehand which method of payment is preferred by both the hire firm and the bridal couple. If it is by paying the driver on the day, the best man should ensure that the groom has given him a cheque to do so and should obtain a receipt.

WEDDING CLOTHES

Unlike the bridesmaids, the best man has to provide his own clothing. Conventionally, this would be a smart suit with a shirt and tie which complements the groom's choice of attire. However, many brides and grooms feel that they would like their special day to have that extra hint of class. They opt for the principal men – groom, groom's father and brothers, best man, ushers, bride's father and brothers, and any others who wish to enter into the spirit of the occasion – to wear top hat and tails (morning suits), or other appropriate formal dress (such as kilts).

Hiring suits

As most people would not want to go to the expense of buying such clothing just for one day, they will want to

hire them. It is likely that the groom will foot the bill
for all the outfits for his side of the family. However, if
the wedding is on a tight budget, the best man and
ushers may hire their own suits so the groom can afford
to be married in style (see 'The groom', p. 224). The
best man is responsible for finding a suitable hire firm
and arranging a convenient time for all concerned to go
for a fitting. Then he will organize payment, time of
delivery and the return of the suits after the ceremony.
It is important that he makes very clear arrangements,
as many hire firms operate on a 24-hour basis. It would
be tactless in the extreme to hire clothing that has to be
back before the very end of the formal reception, thus
requiring the leading men to change their clothes too
early or having to pay for an extra day's hire, just when
they should be enjoying the occasion.

THE SPEECH

So far, the best man's responsibilities have been
confined to making arrangements for others. Now, in
good time for the ceremony, he must turn his attention
to what will be a focal point of the reception – his
speech. Many men will find this prospect daunting; but
by following a few simple rules, the best man will be
able to compose and deliver a speech which will be
remembered as a highlight of the day.

Keeping it short

First, it should be kept short. The guests will have heard
speeches from the bride's father and the groom, and
will be restless if the best man's looks as though it
might be a lengthy affair.

Making it humorous
It should be humorous, but the best man should make
sure it is not in bad taste and should avoid, for example,
making jokes about the groom's past success with
women. A few suitable topics are listed below.

Suitable topics
- How lucky the groom is to have found his bride
- How he and his friends are glad to get the groom off
  their hands
- The performance in getting the groom ready for
  his wedding

The speech should end with a toast to the happy couple.
(See also 'Toasts and speeches', pp. 302-3)

THE STAG NIGHT
One of the traditional pre-wedding rituals is the
groom's 'stag' party, so-called because he invites only
male guests to celebrate his forthcoming marriage and
to commiserate on the loss of his single status.
Depending on the wishes of the groom, this party could
be a small group of close relatives and/or friends going
for a meal, or a larger gathering in a pub or a hall.
Finding out what the groom would like
It is probably one of the best man's more pleasurable
duties to arrange the stag night. First, he will need to
find out what is required, either from the groom or from
his close relatives or friends if it is to be a surprise.
Then he should find out the preferred date.
When to have the stag night
Traditionally, it has been on the wedding eve; but
nowadays, it is some days before. This is because the

event usually involves a certain amount of drinking, and the time lapse gives the groom the chance to get over it before the wedding day itself. If the groom insists on celebrating the night before, then the best man has the task of getting him home in a fit state to face his wedding. The best man can be sure that he, as well as the groom, will incur the wrath of the bride (and her mother) if the groom is not feeling fit on the day.

THE WEDDING REHEARSAL

The wedding rehearsal allows the bridal couple and their attendants to practise the stages of the ceremony with the clergyman (if it is a church wedding), so as to avoid any uncertainties on the day.

Attending the rehearsal

The best man must attend the wedding rehearsal, along with the bride, groom and chief bridesmaid. He has specific duties to perform – keeping the ring, organizing the order of procession to the vestry and the recession afterwards down the aisle. He will need to know the layout of the church. The clergyman will advise him of where he is to stand and the best way for the procession to move if, for example, the church has two aisles.

On the day

BEFORE THE CEREMONY

Finally the wedding day arrives and the best man must be prepared for a hectic time.

Buttonholes, service sheets and messages

Early in the day, the best man collects the buttonholes and the service sheets from the bride's mother. He gives them to the ushers to take to the church and distribute to

the guests. Any telemessages or greetings cards sent to
the bride's or groom's home should be collected by the
best man for reading out at the reception.

The ring and the groom

The best man's most important task is to have the
bride's wedding ring securely in his possession. Then
he must get the groom to the church, properly attired.
The groom should always arrive first, so the best man
should arrange for his car, if any, to bring them to the
church or register office about 20–30 minutes before
the start of the ceremony.

Organizing the ushers

If the wedding is in church, the ushers should have
arrived there an hour or so before the ceremony. Prior
to this, the groom and the best man should have met
with them (see 'The groom', p. 227). At this point, the
best man makes sure the ushers know what they have to
do, and he issues them with seating plans, which he will
have sorted out at the rehearsal.

THE CEREMONY

During the ceremony itself, the best man is one of the
principal players. He delivers the ring to the groom and
he follows the bridal couple into the vestry and signs
the register as a witness to the marriage. He follows the
couple down the aisle, usually with the chief
bridesmaid, and then directs the photographer who
usually begins to take pictures once the couple gets to
the church door. The best man must make sure that the
photographs do not take too long, and that the guests
are aware of their transport arrangements in order to get
to the reception on time. He then leaves for the

reception with the bridesmaids in the second car, after
the bridal couple.

At the register office
If the wedding takes place at a registry office, the best
man will perform the same duties, but also act as a
witness to the marriage in front of the registrar.

AT THE RECEPTION
Duties before the meal
At the reception, the best man will organize a
welcoming party for the bridal couple, direct and time
the photographer, and also organize the ushers to direct
the guests to their seats. He should also take charge of
any wedding presents offered to the couple in the
receiving line and place them on an adjoining side
table. He may also be required to direct guests to the
receiving line, unless there is a Master of Ceremonies.

Introducing the speeches
Once the meal is under way, the best man should keep
an eye on proceedings and judge the time. When the
guests are near the end of their meal, he should stand up
and introduce the speeches (see 'Toasts and speeches',
p. 297). After he has spoken, he reads out all the
telemessages and greetings to the bridal couple. He then
proposes a toast and invites the couple to cut the cake.
After this, the formal setting usually breaks up as guests
mingle to chat or, if there is music, to dance.

AT THE END OF THE DAY
The best man can afford to relax and enjoy the
festivities for a few hours, taking care only to keep an
eye on the time for the bridal couple to leave.

Helping the newlyweds to leave
He makes sure that the couple's car has arrived (see
p. 188) to take them away, that they have any travel
documents for the honeymoon, that the groom's case is
stowed safely and that his discarded wedding suit is
packed ready to return home or to the hirer's.

Decorating the couple's car
The traditional decorating of the groom's car with 'just
married' notices, confetti, balloons or old tin cans may
be supervised by the best man, who should restrain

Best man's checklist
Before the day

- Meet the bride and her family; sort out responsibilities
- Confirm the bridal couple's arrangements with the place of marriage and arrange payment of fees
- Check parking facilities at the place of marriage and reception venue; inform bride's mother so she can advise guests
- Offer to arrange transport for those guests without cars
- If groom's family is paying for the cars, obtain quotations and make arrangements with the hire firm; confirm method of payment; ensure groom provides a cheque if payment is on the day
- If morning dress is to be worn, obtain quotations and arrange hire for groom's side of the family, yourself and ushers. Confirm who is to pay
- Arrange the stag night and look after the groom
- Attend the wedding rehearsal
- Write your speech

more adventurous decorations from crossing the line from good to bad taste.

Bringing the celebrations to a close

Finally, it is the best man who is responsible for bringing the celebrations to a close and making sure that the transport arrangements he made for all the guests go according to plan and everyone has a lift home. He may have to order taxis for those who have been drinking, although it is not his responsibility to ensure drinkers do not drive.

On the day

- Make sure the bride's ring is safe and available
- Obtain buttonholes from the bride's mother
- Make sure the groom arrives at the church or place of marriage in good time
- Organize the ushers and make sure they know the seating plans
- Attend the groom throughout the marriage service
- Organize the photographer and make sure everyone leaves for the reception on time
- Keep proceedings running to time when guests arrive at the reception
- Judge the time to introduce the speeches
- Deliver your speech and read out the greetings
- Propose a toast to the bridal couple
- Make sure the couple leave the reception for their honeymoon on time
- Take care of groom's wedding outfit
- Bring celebrations to a close; make sure everyone has a lift home

HISTORY OF THE BEST MAN'S ROLE
Traditions
Traditionally best men, like bridesmaids, were meant to
be unmarried; today, however, they are as likely to be
married men as bachelors. Historically, the person
fulfilling this role was called the 'brideman' and, later,
the 'groomsman'; whatever he was called, he was
always expected to be the groom's closest friend.
Sometimes this was a brother. Centuries ago, the best
man and ushers sometimes helped the groom steal his
bride and then stood watch to ensure the marriage was
consummated without interruption from the bride's
family; once consummated, the marriage was then
considered to be final.

Superstitions
For the superstitious, some beliefs about the role of the
best man still survive. He is responsible for much of the
future good luck of the newlyweds and, to carry out this
duty, he must make sure the groom carries a small
mascot of some sort in his pocket on the wedding day,
he must not let the groom go back for anything once he
has started out for the church, and he must also make
sure to pay any fees that are required on the day.

COPING WITH EMERGENCY SITUATIONS
Fortunately, most of the mishaps which tend to occur at
weddings are minor irritations rather than major
problems. Minor irritations, such as a ring which has
been mislaid, or an organist who arrives late at the
church, can be easily dealt with, but more serious
problems – such as the theft of the wedding presents
from the reception, or the non-arrival of the live

entertainment – will require much greater skill to resolve. The key to success in any of these emergency situations is anticipation, and having well-thought out, and easily-actionable, contingency plans.

At the ceremony

A late bride

The bride may be late for a number of reasons: the car may not start, heavy traffic or a road accident may have caused a problem, or the chauffeur may even have gone to the wrong church or register office. A simple telephone call by the best man either to the place where the bride is preparing for the ceremony – which may not necessarily be her own home – or to the hire car – if she is using one, and it has a mobile phone! – should put his mind at rest. The organist can be asked to play some impromptu music, or the ushers requested to talk to the wedding guests, so that the delay passes without too much comment.

A misplaced wedding ring

The wedding ring – or, more accurately, its absence, can also cause problems. The best man should make sure it is kept in a safe place prior to the exchange of rings during the ceremony. He should also make sure that the ring is insured, and check whether or not the jeweller could provide a similar ring (of nominal value) in the case of an emergency.

In the case of a Jewish marriage, the ceremony may be invalid if the ring belongs neither to the groom or his family. In such a situation it is often wise for the mother of the groom to wear a ring which can be used during the ceremony and then replaced at a later, more convenient, time.

A non-attendant organist

If the organist fails to turn up because of sickness or some other unexpected mishap, the best man should have the telephone number of a replacement musician at hand. Alternatively, there may be one of the guests who can play the organ and is prepared to help out.

Noisy children

Babies and toddlers often cry, scream, or make other noises during the ceremony. This is only natural and, assuming that the ushers have been warned well in advance, any such potential disturbance should be kept to a mimimum. Guests with babies and toddlers can be offered seats near the aisle, and preferably near the back of the church, so as to facilitate a quick, and relatively unimpeded, exit.

At the reception

Running out of drinks

If the reception has been booked to take place in the function room of a public house or in a hotel, there should be no danger of a drink shortage. The quantity of alcohol likely to be consumed per person – including welcome refreshments, wine with the meal, and suitable drinks for the toasts – are usually planned well in advance. So, unless there are guests with extremely unusual tastes, there should not be a problem.

Receptions at home, or in a private hall for example, can be more difficult to plan. The best man should be prepared to stay sober, or else to make sure he has the telephone number of a friend close at hand – or even of a local off licence – who would be prepared to deliver emergency supplies at short notice!

Shortage of staff

The best man should also make sure that the caterer fully understands whether the couple want a formal, sit-down meal, or an informal, stand-up buffet. This may sound obvious, but misunderstandings of this kind have been known to happen in the past. If confusion does arise, he will probably be called upon to sort it out and, if additional staff cannot be found at short notice, he may have to draft in the ushers, or any other willing guests, as temporary serving staff.

A misplaced speech

Printed copies of speeches – and, by the same token, duplicates – can easily be mislaid during the hectic activity preceeding the reception. It is therefore advisable for both the best man and the groom to rehearse what they intend to say as many times as possible before the actual day itself. The shorter the speech, the easier it will be to remember!

Stolen wedding presents

In order to assist the police shortly after the theft of the wedding presents, or to claim compensation from the insurance company at a later date, the best man should keep a list of all the presents and their estimated value. Cheques are less of a problem as long as the relevant banks are notified as soon as possible.

Non-arrival of the entertainers

In anticipation that the live entertainment may not turn up – their transport may break down, or they may have double-booked the evening – the best man should make sure there is a back-up system, such as cassette tapes or records and a suitable public address system, which is readily available.

17. The bridesmaids

Roles and responsibilities
Before the day

The bridesmaids
- Help with choosing their own clothing
- Attend fitting for dresses, shoes and headdresses

The chief bridesmaid
- Helps the bride to choose her wedding outfit
- Organizes the hen party

On the day: at the church

The bridesmaids
- Arrive at the bride's house to dress and to find out what to do
- Go to the church ahead of the bride

The chief bridesmaid
- With the bride's mother, organizes the other bridesmaids
- Arranges the bride's dress and train on her arrival at the church or register office
- Holds the bride's bouquet during the ceremony
- May have to sign the marriage register
- Helps the bride into her car

On the day: at the reception

The bridesmaids
- Assist the best man in welcoming the bridal couple and the guests
- Offer the wedding cake to the guests

The chief bridesmaid
- Helps to receive the guests

- Assists the bride to change into her going-away outfit
- Brings the bride's bouquet for her to throw into the crowd
- Returns her own and the bridesmaids' outfits, if hired

The bridesmaids play their most important part at the bride's entrance into the church or register office. Their prime function is to be decorative and to add a hint of pageantry to a wedding occasion. They can, however, be of immense help to the bride once they have been chosen. The chief bridesmaid (or matron of honour), if one is appointed, has the very important task of assisting the bride in her choice of dress – for herself and her attendants.

The bride's responsibility: before the day

CHOOSING THE BRIDESMAIDS

Traditionally, bridesmaids are chosen from close, unmarried relatives or friends. It is tactful if there are to be several attendants to ask some of the groom's sisters or cousins to take on the role. If the wedding is large and formal, then the bride might choose to have up to eight attendants, whether bridesmaids or pageboys. A smaller event will require fewer, as too many attendants will look disproportionate to the number of guests.

CHOOSING PAGEBOYS AND FLOWERGIRLS

Pageboys

If the bride – or groom – has small brothers or nephews and would like to include them in the wedding party, then a pageboy, or two, is the answer. Having pageboys is not uncommon, and there are many styles of outfit to choose from in bridal shops and department stores. The boys should be no older than eight, otherwise they should be ushers. The position is generally given to a very small boy, of about five years old, to complement a small bridesmaid of similar age.

Flowergirls

The bride might like to have smaller relatives as bridesmaids. She may be nervous, though, of giving them the responsibility of being the centre of attention during the ceremony, as they may have to stand still and silent for the better part of an hour. So rather than disappoint them, the bride could compromise by appointing very small girls as flower-bearers, who will perhaps scatter petals in front of her as she walks up the aisle (check with the clergyman first), or who will follow the bridal party, holding posies of flowers.

During the ceremony

When the bride reaches the groom and the party stands for the ceremony, the flowergirls can go to their parents in the congregation until the recession, when they may join the party for the walk back down the aisle and for the photographs.

CHOOSING THE CHIEF BRIDESMAID

By convention, the bride has at least one, chief, bridesmaid, who will help her dress on the morning of

the wedding, carry her train up the aisle and hold her
bouquet during the marriage ceremony. She may even
be called upon to sign the register if she is over 18.
Therefore, the role of chief bridesmaid should go to
someone able to fulfil these functions with the
minimum of fuss. Usually an adult sister, cousin or
close friend – or the groom's adult sister if the bride has
none – is a perfect choice. Whoever is chosen,
however, must be old enough to take on these duties.

Making a suitable choice

Anyone younger than 16 is likely to feel overburdened,
and a small girl is a very unwise choice for this
position, even if she might be the bride's only sister.
Therefore the bride should decide quickly if an obvious
choice is likely to falter on the day, and explain to her
at the outset the reason why someone else has been
chosen. Initial disappointment will always give way to
excitement as the wedding nears if the bride has been
honest.

Matron of honour

If the bride's choice of chief bridesmaid is married,
then she is called the matron of honour, 'matron' being
a traditional term for a married woman. Her duties are
exactly the same as her unmarried counterpart, but the
bride is likely to choose a different style of dress for her
to wear.

If the role is refused

Although it is usually considered an honour to be a
bridesmaid, there are occasions when someone has to
refuse. This could be because of a prior engagement.
Sometimes, though, a person knows she will feel
uncomfortable in the limelight, and that being a

prominent member of the wedding party would spoil
the whole day for her. The bride should try to be
understanding, if this happens, and cover her own
disappointment – the prime objective of the occasion is
for everyone to be happy.

DRESSING THE BRIDESMAIDS
Who pays?
Choice of outfits for the bridesmaids very much
depends on who is paying for the dresses – and the
accessories. If the bride's parents are paying for the
wedding, the bride will normally choose the
bridesmaids' outfits, and either the bride or her parents
will foot the bill. However, the parents of those chosen
(if different from the bride's) may offer to contribute all
or part of the cost of the dresses. If so, then it is fair to
consult the bridesmaids in question before making the
final choice.

Choosing the style
This choice will depend on several factors. The most
straightforward is a style and colour of dresses that will
complement the bride. If the bride is in a long,
elaborate gown, then her bridesmaids can be similarly
attired. If, however, she has decided to marry in a knee-
length, smart suit or dress – if the bride is an older
woman or marrying for the second time, for example –
then she might feel that beribboned, flowing dresses on
her bridesmaids will look fussy and out-of-place.
Certainly, a matron of honour should not be dressed in
frills and flounces, although this sort of dress always
looks charming on very small girls.

Choosing a style to suit all

A bride who has chosen several bridesmaids of different ages, heights, sizes and colouring has the complicated task of choosing a style and colour to suit them all. An off-the-shoulder design may flatter her adult sisters, but will look in extremely poor taste on a girl under 16. Conversely, little-girl dresses do nothing for a grown woman. Similarly, a full skirt with a pinched-in waist will look ungainly on a bridesmaid who is of large build.

Choosing the colour

The choice of style is limitless, but colours are not. Most brides choose pastels – blue, pink, lemon, lilac (not green, it is widely considered to be unlucky) – which always flatter a pure white dress. But there is no convention against choosing brighter colours, such as deep pink, red, purple or even orange, particularly if the bride herself has opted for a bold colour for her own dress, but lurid hues may overpower the traditional bridal white. As a compromise, the bride who wants her wedding party to be stylish may opt for a 'safe' overall colour for her bridesmaids' dresses, but trim them with the striking colours she feels will bring originality to the occasion.

Choosing a colour to suit all

A careful choice should also be made where the bridesmaids have vastly differing colouring. For example, a strong, sunshine yellow that looks stunning on a girl with raven hair and olive skin will make a peaches-and-cream-skinned blonde look insipid.

Ordering the dresses

Once the bride has settled on her choice, then she has

almost the same decisions to make as she had with her own dress. Will she buy, hire or make? Whatever the final choice, she must do so in sufficient time for fittings and alterations to be made. She will have to take into consideration the ease with which her chosen bridesmaids can attend fittings – perhaps some are out at work during the week, or live a considerable distance away. They should all come together at least once before the wedding day.

Accessories

As with her own ensemble, the bride will need to give careful consideration to the bridesmaids' headdresses, if any, as well as shoes and flowers. Colour and style are important, as a certain headdress may not suit all age-groups and each individual's colouring. With shoes, there may be more choice. They can be formal, light- or matching-coloured court shoes or sandals for the adults, and sandals or soft shoes (ballet pumps, for example) for the very young ones.

Ordering the headdresses

Once she has decided, the bride can order headdresses, flowers and shoes (at the same time she orders her own) to be delivered to the address from which she is to be married. It makes sense for the bridesmaids to dress at this venue instead of wearing their outfits from their own homes. Apart from helping to prevent creasing, it will give all those taking part a chance to make any last-minute adjustments.

The bridesmaids' roles:
before the day

THE HEN NIGHT

As well as helping the bride with her choice of outfits, for herself and her attendants, the chief bridesmaid could take on the responsibility for organizing the bride's hen night. On this occasion, the bride invites her female friends and relatives to celebrate her impending marriage and also to have one last 'taste of freedom'.

On the day

BEFORE THE CEREMONY

On the morning of the wedding, all attendants should meet the bride at her mother's house (or from where she is to leave for the ceremony) in good time to dress and to organize themselves. The chief bridesmaid (or the bride's mother) should take charge and tell the others what they will be expected to do, as she will have been told at the wedding rehearsal earlier in the week. The duties of the matron of honour are identical.

THE CEREMONY
Looking after the bride

The chief bridesmaid will travel to the church, or register office, with the other attendants in advance of the bride and her father. Once there, they will all welcome the bride on her arrival, but the chief bridesmaid should help her alight from the car (or carriage) and arrange her dress and veil. If the bride's dress has a train, the chief bridesmaid helps to carry it to the church door. She then arranges the train on the floor, so it glides attractively behind the bride, whom she follows up the aisle. The other bridesmaids and pageboys follow, often in twos and in order of decreasing age. As the bride draws level with her groom and stops, so does her retinue. The chief bridesmaid takes the bride's bouquet and lifts her veil.

Signing the register
All attendants stand by as the ceremony progresses, then all or just the chief bridesmaid (or matron of honour) follow the newly married couple into the vestry where the marriage register is signed. The chief bridesmaid, if legally of age, may sign the register as one of the two witnesses needed.

Leaving the church
The bridal party walks down the aisle. After giving the bride her bouquet, the chief bridesmaid partners the best man (see 'Church weddings', pp. 101-3).

At the register office
At a register office wedding, there are likely to be fewer attendants, due to pressure of space – marriage rooms may accommodate only up to 30 or 40 people. Most brides, however, will have a chief bridesmaid or matron of honour, and her duties are exactly the same as for a church wedding. There is no room for a procession, but the wedding party may enter and leave the room in the same order as they would do in church.

AT THE RECEPTION
The welcoming party
The chief bridesmaid once again travels with the other attendants, and organizes them into a welcoming party

for the bridal couple. The chief bridesmaid may help
the best man seat the guests; but, primarily, she should
help the bride to take her place.

Gifts from the bridegroom

After his speech, the groom traditionally presents each
of the bridesmaids with a small gift, such as jewellery,
as a token of his appreciation of their service to his
bride (see 'The groom', pp. 225 and 229).

Offering cake to the guests

Then, the guests are usually delighted to be offered
their portions of wedding cake by the other bridesmaids
(and pageboys) who take round the plates, unless this is
done by waiters and waitresses.

Helping the bride to change

After this, the bridesmaids may relax and enjoy the
occasion. The chief bridesmaid, though, should be on
hand to help the bride out of her wedding dress and into
her going-away outfit prior to the couple leaving. She
should also hand the bride her bouquet at the very last
minute for her to throw into the crowd as she departs.

Clearing up

If the reception is at the hosts' home, or in a hired hall,
she and the others could help the bride's mother clear
up the debris. But if caterers are involved, they will
have their own personnel to see to clearing the room.

Returning hired clothes

The chief bridesmaid should take charge of returning
any hired bridesmaids' outfits, making sure she does so
before the hire time expires.

Overleaf are checklists for the bride, the bridesmaids
and the chief bridesmaid/matron of honour.

Bride's checklist
- Choose bridesmaids carefully, bearing in mind what they will be expected to do on the day
- Try to draw an even balance between your relatives and those of the groom, if there are to be several bridesmaids
- Ensure that the style and colour of the dresses complement the bridal gown and suit all the bridesmaids. Allow the bridesmaids to voice their own preferences before making a final decision
- Order the attendants' costumes in sufficient time to allow for fittings and for people travelling long distances
- Try to get all the attendants together at least once before the wedding day
- Make sure each knows her (or his) own duties for the day

Bridesmaids' checklist
Before the day

- Before accepting the role of bridesmaid, make sure that you know what the responsibilities will be
- If given a say in the choice of dress, bear in mind the overall effect the bride is trying to create, not just your favourite fashion
- Attend any fittings needed for the dress, shoes and headdress

On the day

- Arrive at the bride's house in good time to find out what to do and to dress
- At the church, keep calm and know where you

are meant to stand and what you are meant to do
- Assist the best man in welcoming the bridal couple
- Offer the wedding cake to the guests

Chief bridesmaid (or matron of honour)
Before the day

- Before accepting the role of chief bridesmaid or matron of honour, ensure that you know the responsibilities, and remember that the bride will depend upon you for support
- Organize the hen night
- Assist the bride in her purchase of her wedding outfit

On the day

- Help the bride dress
- Arrange her dress and train (if there is one) on her arrival at the church or register office
- Hold the bride's bouquet during the marriage ceremony and return it after the register has been signed
- Be prepared to sign the marriage register as a witness, if asked
- Help the bride into her car for the journey to the reception and help receive the guests there
- Assist the bride in dressing in her going-away outfit
- Bring the bride's bouquet for her to throw into the crowd
- If required, help the bride's mother to clear up
- Return the dresses, if they have been hired

18. The ushers

Roles and responsibilities
Before the day

- Find out what you will be wearing

On the day: before the ceremony

- Arrive an hour before the guests are due to arrive
- Ensure the clergyman has a service sheet
- Hand out hymn books and service sheets to guests
- Offer guests a buttonhole, if provided
- Show guests to their seats
- Guide the bride's mother to her seat

On the day: the church

- Deal with latecomers and disturbances
- Assist the best man in making sure all the guests get to the reception on time

In many ways, the ushers are the 'unsung heroes' of the wedding day. Their job is to organize the guests, both at the church (or the register office) and the reception, so discreetly that they might almost be invisible.

Deciding if ushers are required

Unless the wedding is quite small, someone should have the sole duty of making sure the guests are in the right place at the right time. Ushers are not so essential at a register office, as the marriage room – and numbers of guests – should be small enough to be managed by

the best man. However, in churches, which usually
have more seats than guests, or where the wedding
party numbers over 30 people, ushers are invaluable.
For example, several people will be needed to seat
perhaps 70 or 80 guests who converge on the church 10
minutes before the ceremony begins. In the rush,
mistakes can made, and it is up to the ushers to solve
any problems. They are responsible for sorting out
seating mistakes and deflecting the possibility of guests
arguing over who sits where.

The bridal couple's reponsibility: before the day

CHOOSING THE USHERS

The bride and groom should envisage four as the ideal
number of ushers to manage their guests. Traditionally,
the honour is given to the bride's brothers, and perhaps
a second brother of the groom if another has been
chosen as best man. Cousins also can perform these
duties. Choosing the ushers from both sides of the
family means that, collectively, they will recognize
most of the guests, which will make their job a great
deal easier.

Making a suitable choice

The ushers, ideally, should have a flair for organization,
and so should be adults. It would be unfair to choose a
young boy out of sentiment if he is likely to be
overwhelmed by the sheer weight of his task. Showing
people to their seats might not look too taxing, but it
does require some degree of skill.

The ushers's roles: before the day

WHAT TO WEAR

The ushers are regarded as 'leading men' on the wedding day, and so should dress formally.

Morning dress

If the groom has opted for morning dress, then it is his duty to provide suits for his ushers (see 'The groom', p. 224). As morning suits tend to be indistinguishable, the ushers might wear a flower buttonhole of a different colour from the groom's and the best man's. This will avoid confusion, say, when the photographer is assembling people for his pictures.

Lounge or dinner suits

If the groom is getting married in a lounge or dinner suit, then the ushers should wear the same. As most people own at least one suit, the groom is not obliged to provide them. The ushers, however, should check with the groom what colour shirt and tie he is wearing, and try to dress differently in this regard, to avoid confusion of identity. An usher should *not* upstage the groom by dressing in a way that puts the latter in the shade.

On the day

BEFORE THE CEREMONY

Meeting with the best man and the groom

The leading men meet to make sure that everyone knows what to do. At this meeting, the ushers will be given a seating plan, the buttonholes and service sheets, which they must take to the church.

When to get to the church
It is crucial to the smooth running of the occasion that
the ushers are in place well before the expected arrival
of the guests. Proceedings will get off to the worst
possible start if early guests wander into an empty
church and, for the want of guidance, sit in the wrong
place. It may be embarrassing to move them, and if
they refuse to sit elsewhere, then the carefully prepared
seating plan will be in ruins from the outset.
Of course, it is impossible to cater for the arrival of
very early guests, but the ushers should be in position
not later than 45 minutes before the ceremony is due to
start. One hour before would be ideal.

The clergyman's service sheet
It is the responsibility of the chief usher to make sure
the minister has the same service sheet as the
congregation.

THE CEREMONY
How to behave
As the ushers are leading men, it is important that they
conduct themselves in a proper manner. They should
not be seen by approaching guests lounging on
doorways or pillars, or talking amongst themselves.
They should look calm and relaxed, but ready to
perform their duties efficiently.

Where to stand and what to do
If four ushers have been appointed, then a member of
each side of the family should 'look after' his own
relatives inside the church. Two should stand at the
back of the pews (or front, depending on where the
door is) on their respective sides. The two remaining

ushers should position themselves at the door of the church to welcome guests as they approach. They should hand each guest a hymn book and/or buttonhole, if provided (also offering to affix the flower to the guest's clothing). If neither usher at the door recognizes a guest, one should ask whether he or she is 'with the bride or groom', and then direct them to the correct side of the aisle.

Seating plan

Conventionally, the bride's family sits on the left of the aisle, looking towards the altar, while the groom's relatives sit on the right. In addition, the closer the relative, the nearer the front they expect to sit. This usually means friends will sit further back, but not always. The bride or groom may feel that a close friend takes precedence over a distant relative. If the conventional order has changed, it should be indicated on the plan where the conventional order is rearranged.

Seating the guests

The ushers stationed by the pews receive the guests and ask whether they are family or friends, if they do not know already. They will then guide the guests to their allotted seats and make sure they are comfortable.

Positioning guests wisely

This might include positioning guests with babies or disabled guests at the end of pews, or making sure tall people with large hats are not seated in front of small children. The ushers should never show a guest to a position with an obscured view of the altar if a seat with a clear view is available.

Dealing with latecomers

The ushers should have all the guests seated by the time the bride makes her entrance. The last to make her entrance (before the bride) will be the bride's mother. The chief usher should escort her to her place in the front pew, on the left of the aisle. They may breathe a sigh of relief as they watch the bride glide up the aisle, but they must not think their work is over. Invariably, there are latecomers who may hover at the door, uncertain of what to do. The vigilant usher should see that they are provided with a service sheet and flower, and should then show them discreetly to a seat where their arrival will not disrupt the ceremony. The ushers must use the utmost tact – but be firm – in dissuading an anxious close relative from jostling through a packed pew and causing a disturbance.

Dealing with disturbances

Similarly, if a guest has a young baby which starts to cry, an usher should discreetly offer to help her from her place to a side room or out of the door. He must resist the temptation to offer to look after the child, as he will not be able to attend to his duties if he does.

Leaving the church

Traditionally, the ushers follow the bridesmaids in the recessional down the aisle (see pp. 102-3). Once out of the church, they can help the photographer by finding the relevant guests for his pictures. Afterwards, they should assist the best man in ensuring that all the guests make their way to the reception at the appointed time. If this is some distance away, then they will also help the best man in seeing to it that everyone has transport.

AT THE RECEPTION

The ushers guide the guests to the reception room and receiving line, and (if applicable) to their seats. This will be a much easier task, as the guests' names will be at their places, and also there is not so much concern about time. Once the meal is under way, the ushers can relax and enjoy the proceedings.

Ushers' checklist
On the day: at the place of marriage

- Meet with the groom and the best man
- Arrive at the church in good time
- Make sure you have the seating plan, order of service sheets or hymn books, and buttonholes for the guests, if provided
- Decide where each of you will stand
- Welcome each guest individually; provide each one with a service sheet and flower
- Ask if they are with the bride or groom
- Guide the guests to their seats, according to the seating plan
- Ensure no one has an obscured view
- Welcome latecomers and seat them discreetly
- Help guests in difficulty, e.g. a mother with a crying baby
- Participate in the recessional
- Assist the photographer by finding relatives and friends for his pictures
- Help make sure guests depart for the reception on time and that they have transport

At the reception

- Assist with seating the guests

19. Appendices

Appendix A: Insurance

With all the attention to detail while organizing a
wedding, it is easy to overlook the possibility of
catastrophes which are beyond anyone's control.
Therefore it is advisable to obtain insurance cover.

WHICH INSURANCE?
Wedding insurance is a specialized area. An insurance
broker will know which firms offer cover and will
advise you of the best deal. This is preferable to
embarking on the task of ringing round a number of
companies.

Cost
In comparison with the cost of the occasion, the
premiums for wedding insurance are relatively small.

Compensation for cancellation
Cancellation compensation will usually be given if
caused by death, accident, illness, compulsory
quarantine, court summons, jury service or
unemployment (provided this occurred through
redundancy, as defined by the Government) after the
date the policy was issued.

WHAT IS COVERED?
Typical cover offered by one of the larger companies
in this area of insurance includes cancellation, retaking
photographs, replacing wedding attire and presents,
and public liability.

Reception hall

If the place booked for the reception cannot
accommodate the function because of fire, damage,
murder or suicide occurring on the premises, outbreak
of contagious diseases, or even closure by the local
authority, such as on grounds of health, then the bride
and groom can claim the cost of rebooking elsewhere.

Sudden closure of the hall

In some cases, the whole day may have to be cancelled
because of sudden closure of the premises (and the
impossibility of booking another venue at such short
notice). Such an event could entail fresh church or
register office fees, the cost of dress hire, car hire, the
photographer and various other expenses. The bride and
groom should bear this in mind when assessing the
value of cover they want.

No cover for marquees

Some insurance policies do not allow for compensation
due to cancellation caused by damage to a marquee or
other outdoor location of a similar nature. This is likely
to be because damage could be sustained as a result of a
preventable occurrence – faulty erection or inadequate
fire equipment, for example.

Wedding attire

Some cover also includes cancellation as a result of
damage to wedding attire – bride's and bridesmaids'
dresses and accessories, and men's hired suits. Some
policies, however, exclude claims for damage to
accessories, such as the bride's headdress, if the dress
itself has not been damaged. Also, there is usually a
proviso that the damage must have occurred within five
working days of the wedding and that every effort must

have been made to replace the damaged items. Again, when assessing the level of cover they require, the couple should take into consideration the cost of other items (such as marriage fees, the reception and the photographer, not just the cost to replace damaged outfits), if the whole wedding has to be cancelled.

If the wedding does not have to be cancelled
When damage to bridal wear does not necessitate the cancellation of the wedding, the couple can still insure and receive compensation for its replacement.

The photographer and the photographs
Insurance can be taken out against the photographer not turning up on the day, or against loss of, damage to or non-development of their wedding photographs. Cover would include any hire expenses or additional costs which would have to be met to create the same effect for the pictures to be retaken.

Wedding presents
Often these are the most obvious worry, if presents are kept overnight at the reception hall, ready to display to the guests on the day, or if they are left in the couple's empty house while they are on honeymoon. Most reception halls' and home-owners' contents policies may provide cover, but the limit may not be sufficient to meet a claim. Having special insurance would mean peace of mind and one less worry.

Public liability
Most policies will automatically cover the insured for public liability – in the event of prosecution or suit for damages as a result of injury to a guest or damage to their property. The sums insured in these cases are always huge.

Bad weather

Cancellation due to unforeseen circumstances does not
normally include the weather – if it rains heavily and a
proposed garden party has to be cancelled, for example.
Some specialized insurers will offer separate cover, but
the premiums vary as these will depend on the
circumstances of the wedding and the time of year at
which it is to take place. But a premium for insurance
against rain in July will be far less than for November.

WHO IS COVERED?

Cover can be for the bride or groom or their parents,
and it may also be provided by some policies if any one
of them is called away suddenly overseas as a result of
their occupation – as may happen with someone in the
armed services, for example.

Appendix B: Toasts and speeches

One of the most daunting prospects for the groom, best
man and bride's father at the wedding is the speech
each traditionally makes after the meal at the reception.
All three main speakers fear that they will appear as
tongue-tied amateurs, but this is unlikely to happen if
some simple guidelines are followed.

It is not compulsory, however, for any of the 'leading
men' to make a speech, especially if they feel having to
do so would ruin the day.

WHO SHOULD SPEAK?

Traditionally, it is the bride's father, the groom and the
best man who make the speeches. Women were, in the
past, considered too modest to draw attention to

themselves. But there are no hard and fast rules on who
may speak – only conventions. If, say, the bride's father
feels too nervous to speak, an uncle or brother can step
in. And if the groom is convinced he will make a fool
of himself, there is nothing to stop the bride from
addressing her guests.

WHO INTRODUCES THE SPEECHES?

If there is no toastmaster, the best man performs these
duties. He judges when the speeches should start,
perhaps as the guests are finishing the dessert course of
their meal, and then he calls each speaker in turn.

ORDER OF SPEAKERS

There are at least three speakers who rise in the
following order:
- the bride's father;
- the groom; and
- the best man.

PURPOSES OF THE SPEECHES

Once the leading men have agreed to make the
traditional speeches, they must treat the task seriously,
giving thought to the content and delivery of the
speech. Very few people can rise and speak off-the-cuff
without preparation. An inexperienced speaker takes
the risk of rambling off the point, boring the guests and
fulfilling his own prophecy of being no good at public
speaking.

Essential elements

The speaker concerned should first fix in his mind on
the purpose of his speech, which is to thank people,
propose toasts, or reply to other speeches. The rest is

embroidery. If all a nervous speaker can manage are these simple courtesies, that is good enough. But most speakers will want to entertain the guests a little, in which case an order of topics to be covered should be written down.

Avoiding ready-made speeches

On no account should the speaker buy a book of ready-made speeches and learn one parrot-fashion; it will sound false and stilted. There is no substitute for his own sentiments, however modest. It is a good idea for the speaker to put himself in the place of a guest, and to remember what he would like to hear in a speech.

PREPARING THE SPEECHES

Delivery

Delivery of the speeches is just as important as their content. There is nothing worse than a long, rambling address which is mumbled and stammered through. Therefore, it would be wise for the speaker to be prepared in order to avoid these pitfalls.

Duration

Each speech should last no more than four or five minutes. Three speeches, plus toasts, will then last about 20 minutes, enough for the most patient guest's attention span. Once the speech has been written out, the speaker should time himself and prune his remarks to fit the time limit. But he should be careful about the speed at which he reads aloud. There is little point in the speaker racing ahead to cram in all his remarks, otherwise the whole speech will be too fast for the guests to take any of it in.

Mirror practice
A good way of measuring the pace and length of a
speech is to recite it in front of a mirror. Not only will
this perfect its delivery, it will also alert the speaker to
any mannerisms, such as twitching or shuffling, which
may annoy guests and attract more attention than the
speech. Seeing himself perform in this way, the speaker
can practise being conversational and relaxed.

Memorizing opening words and linking phrases
The speaker might find it helpful to write the main
points of his speech on prompt cards. This will make it
seem a little more chatty and spontaneous, which may
be preferable to just reading it. He will be talking to the
guests: so it would be an idea for him to memorize his
opening words, and some linking phrases so that he can
look up from his notes and make eye-contact with his
audience, particularly with anyone who is mentioned.

THE BRIDE'S FATHER'S SPEECH
About his daughter
The bride's father might order his speech in the
following way. He might begin by talking about the
happiness he and his wife experienced in bringing up
such a fine daughter. This will give him an opportunity
of relating one or two stories about her early life,
perhaps an amusing anecdote followed by a more
serious one which indicates an (attractive) aspect of her
character.

Welcoming his new son-in-law
Then he might reflect on the loss of a daughter, while
welcoming a new son-in-law and his parents into the
family circle.

Fatherly advice
As his speech should be of a semi-serious nature, the
bride's father is entitled to offer some advice to the
couple as they start their new life. This need not be too
heavy-handed – he could quote a famous person to get
his point across. For example, advice about not being
heartbroken at the first cross word may be supported by
the observation from the writer, A. P. Herbert that:

> The concept of two people living together for
> 25 years without having a cross word suggests a
> lack of spirit only to be admired in sheep.

(There are books of quotations to fit all occasions,
which could give any of the speech-makers inspiration
for a witty remark.)

Suggested contents of the father's speech
- His happiness on bringing up his daughter
- One or two stories, possibly funny, to illustrate the
  sort of person she is
- His daughter beginning her new life
- A welcome to his son-in-law and his parents as
  new members of the family
- An item of advice on the couple's future together

The first toast
The bride's father then proposes the first toast of the
occasion, to the bride and groom. Traditionally,
everyone stands for the toast – except the people being
toasted – but the guests may remain seated if this is
more convenient.

THE GROOM'S SPEECH
It is now the groom's turn to respond to the toast. His

speech is mainly to thank people, and so he is not expected to deliver a witty or entertaining address.

Thanking both sets of parents

The groom should thank the bride's father on behalf of himself and his bride for the toast just proposed. He could also praise the bride's parents on having brought up their daughter so well. He may then continue to thank his parents for their kindness and sacrifices while bringing him up, and possibly respond to any advice given by the bride's father. However, this demands improvisation; so if nothing sensible springs to mind immediately, the subject is best left alone.

The bride and the bridesmaids

An amusing story about meeting his bride, and any difficulties which have been overcome on the way to marriage, would make a diversion from the lists of thanks at this point. His speech should go on to close with thanks to his best man and to the bridesmaids, and anyone else who has helped – relatives who may have helped prepare the food, or made the bridesmaids' dresses, for example. Before proposing a toast to the bridesmaids, the groom may wish to give them some memento of the occasion. This is usually something small and personal, such as perfume or jewellery.

Suggested contents of the groom's speech

- Thanks to the bride's parents and the bridesmaids
- Thanks to his parents
- An amusing story about meeting his bride or their preparations for the wedding
- Thanks to the ushers and the best man
- Thanks to the guests for attending

● Proposing of the toast to the bridesmaids

THE BEST MAN'S SPEECH
Thanking the groom
The best man now rises to thank the groom on behalf of the bridesmaids. As all the necessary thanks and toasts have been given, he is free to continue his speech as he chooses. It usually falls to the best man to entertain the guests with witty observations or funny stories. If the groom has chosen his best man for the ability to deliver such a speech, then he can proceed with all confidence.
Avoiding remarks that are in bad taste
If the best man is not comfortable making such a speech, he should not attempt it. It is far better to keep his remarks short than to try to be funny and risk ruining the occasion with something in bad taste. Just such a *faux pas* would be to try to make a joke of marriage itself, using quotes such as Groucho Marx's

> Marriage is a fine institution, but who wants to live in an institution?

or, in a more literary vein, the poet William Blake's observation:

> When a man marries a woman he finds out whether her elbows and knees are really stuck together.

These may seem funny, but it is almost certain that neither the bride nor her family will see the joke.
Jokes and anecdotes about the groom
It is acceptable to make jokes at the expense of the groom, as long as they are in good taste and do not

include references to his past experiences with women, the honeymoon or baby stories. Safe subjects would include anecdotes revealing the sort of person the groom is, or recounting events leading up to the wedding. It would be gracious for the best man to end his speech by congratulating the groom on his choice of bride, followed by wishes for their future happiness.

Suggested contents of the best man's speech
- Thanks to the groom on behalf of the bridesmaids
- Anecdotes about the groom
- Toast to the bride and groom's future happiness

DELIVERY ON THE DAY

As one of the 'leading men', the speaker will have a lot to remember on the day. He must ensure that his carefully prepared speech is in his pocket before he goes. Even if he has taken the trouble to memorize it, he will feel more confident if he has the text to hand.

Staying sober

The speaker should *never* rely on 'dutch courage'. For him to get drunk to face the audience could end in disaster, and prove embarrassing to all concerned.

Starting the speech

When the speaker's turn comes, he should take a deep breath and rise slowly. It would be wise for him to pause before beginning his speech. This will allow the guests to focus their attention on what he is going to say.

Addressing the guests

The speaker should begin by addressing the guests. The form this takes depends on the formality of the occasion and who is present: for example, 'Ladies and gentlemen' or, simply, 'Relatives and friends'. If someone with a title is present, it is courteous to acknowledge the fact. For example, if a clergyman has been invited, he should be addressed before the others as 'Reverend' or with the usual form of address for his denomination. Earls, dukes, bishops and lords should be addressed as 'my lord'.

Proposing a toast

When the speaker has finished expressing his thanks and his general remarks, he should ask the guests to

---

Toasts and speeches checklists
Preparation before the day

Do
- Write down topics to be covered
- Avoid embarrassing jokes
- Practise the speech
- Write out prompt cards and memorize openings words and linking phrases
- Time the speech
- Control nervous mannerisms

Do not
- Memorize a prepared speech from a book
- Try to impress with over-long or high-sounding sentences

Delivery on the day

Do
- Speak slowly
- Speak out to and make eye contact with the guests
- Be conversational
- Be yourself

raise their glasses in honour of the people he is about to toast. He should wait until everyone is ready – with glasses filled and standing (if this is desired).

Ways of proposing a toast
- I give you the bride and groom
- Here's to the happiness of a beautiful bride and her handsome groom

After the guests have drunk the toast, the speech is at an end and the speaker may sit down.

Do not
- Mumble or race through the speech
- Fidget, sway, shuffle feet or otherwise distract the guests from the speech
- drink too much beforehand

The bride's father

- Speak first
- Propose a toast to the bride and groom

The groom

- Speak after the bride's father, responding to the bride's father
- Propose a toast to the bridesmaids
- Present the bridesmaids with gifts

The best man

- Act as toastmaster: judge when to introduce the bride's father's speech
- Introduce the groom's speech
- Speak after the groom, responding to the groom on behalf of the bridesmaids
- Propose a toast to the bride and groom

Appendix C: Summaries of traditional roles

WHO DOES WHAT

The responsibilities outlined below are those that were (and are) traditionally assumed by certain participants. The bridal couple may manage most of the arrangements themselves, leaving only 'ceremonial duties' for their parents, the best man, and so on. A male relative (or friend) other than the bride's father may also give the bride away, if she prefers. She may, of course, choose to walk up the aisle unescorted.

The bride

- Makes major decisions about the style of the wedding and the reception
- Chooses her bridesmaids/pageboys/flowergirls

The groom

- Sorts out legal arrangements (Certificate and Licence)
- Pays for the ceremony
- Makes the second speech at the reception

The bride's mother

- Acts as wedding hostess
- Sends out the invitations
- Traditionally makes arrangements for the reception
- Is present at the signing of the register
- Is escorted by the groom's father for the recessional

The bride's father

- Escorts the bride to the church and gives her away
- Escorts the groom's mother for the recessional
- Makes first speech at the reception

The best man

- Acts as intermediary between the bride's family and the groom, and keeps everyone informed of the wedding preparations
- Before and on the day aids the groom with arrangements
- Accompanies the groom to the ceremony
- Organizes the ushers

- Looks after the ring and gives it to the groom during the ceremony
- Escorts the chief bridesmaid for the recessional
- At the reception, makes the third speech and reads the messages
- Looks after the honeymoon documents and luggage

The chief bridesmaid/matron of honour

- Helps the bride with all her preparations before the ceremony
- After the reception, helps her to change and looks after the wedding dress

---

Bridesmaids

- Add an attractive element to the proceedings

Ushers

- At the church, greet and seat the guests
- Help with parking arrangements and transport

Groom's parents

- Present for the signing of the register
- Escort, or are escorted by, the bride's parents
- May help to pay for and plan the reception

WHO PAYS FOR WHAT

The financial roles outlined below are those that were (and are) assumed by certain participants. Nowadays, the bridal couple and/or both sets of parents may choose to share all the costs.

Groom's parents

Traditionally, the groom's parents are not involved financially. The increasing cost of getting married, however, means that they may share the expenses with the bride's parents and/or the bridal couple.

Bride's parents

- Hen party
- Stationery, including: invitations (printing and postage); Order of Service sheets; napkins, place cards, cake boxes, etc.
- Clothing, including: bride's dress and accessories (not the bouquet); dresses for the bridesmaids
- Cars/other transport, for the bride's side of the family and her bridesmaids, to church and reception
- Floral decorations for the church and reception
- Music during the ceremony
- Photography/video
- Reception, including: food and drink; venue; caterers; wedding cake; Master of ceremonies (if the best man is not taking on the role); Chauffeurs, catering staff, etc.; music

The groom

- Engagement ring
- Stag party
- Bride's wedding ring
- Buttonholes, corsages, flowers for the bride and her bridesmaids
- Church or civil ceremony fees (not the flowers and the music)
- Legal costs
- Hires clothes for himself, the best man and ushers (if buying the suits, then the best man and ushers can buy their own)
- Car for himself and the best man
- The bride's, best man's and attendants' presents
- The honeymoon and all associated expenses

The bride

- Groom's wedding ring
- Other possible expenses: bridesmaids' presents; wedding dress and going-away outfit

Other than these, the bride (traditionally) has no wedding expenses

Appendix D: Musical Selection

The following pieces of music are popularly chosen for playing at various times during the service.

As the bride arrives

Brahms	*Theme* from the *St Anthony Chorale*
Charpentier	*Prelude to a Te Deum*
Clarke	*Prince of Denmark's March*
Guilmant	*March on Lift up your Heads*
Handel	*Hornpipe in D* from the *Water Music*
	Hornpipe in F from the *Water Music*
	March from *Scipio*
	Coro from the *Water Music*
	Minuet No 2 from the *Water Music*
	Arrival of the Queen of Sheba
	March from the *Occasional Oratorio*
Harris	*Wedding Processional*
Hollins	*A Trumpet Minuet*
Parry	*Bridal March*
Purcell	*Trumpet Tune*
	Rondeau from *Abdelazar*
Verdi	*Grand March* from *Aida*
Wagner	*Bridal March* from *Lohengrin*
Walton	*March* from *Richard III*
	Crown Imperial

For the entrance of the recessional

Boyce	*Trumpet Voluntary*
Bride	*Allegro Marzialle*
Guilmant	*Allegro* from *Sonata in D minor*
Karg-Elert	*Praise the Lord O My Soul*
Mendelssohn	*Sonata No 3* (first movement)
Stanley	*Trumpet Voluntary* from *Suite in D*
Suttle	*Wedding March*
Wesley	*Choral Song*

While the register is being signed

Albinoni	*Adagio in G minor*
Bach	*Air* from *Suite in D*
	Sheep may safely graze
	Adagio from *Toccato Adagio and Fugue*
	Jesu, Joy of Man's Desiring
Brahms	*Behold, a rose is blooming*
Handel	*Minuet* from *Berenice*
	Air from the *Water Music*
Macdowell	*To wild rose*
Mendelssohn	*Allegretto* from *Sonata No 4*
Mozart	*Romanze* from *Ein Kleine Nachtmusik*
Schubert	*Ave Maria*
Schumann	*Traumerei*
Vaughan-Williams	*Chorale prelude on Rhosymedre*
Wesley	*Air* from *Three Pieces*

As the couple leave the church

Guilmant	*Grand Choeur in D*
Fletcher	*Festive Toccata*
Karg-Elert	*Now thank we all our God*
Mendelssohn	*Wedding March* from *A Midsummer Night's Dream*
Mulet	*Carrillon-Sortie*
Smart	*Postlude in D*
Vierne	*Carrillon in B flat*
	Final from *Symphony No 1*
Walton	*Crown Imperial*
Whitlock	*Fanfare*
Widor	*Toccata* from *Symphony No 5*

Appendix E: Menu ideas for buffets

Traditional dishes

- Sausage rolls
- Hard-boiled eggs
- Scotch eggs
- Pâtés
- Egg and cress sandwiches
- Ham sandwiches
- Cucumber and cream cheese rolls
- Salmon sandwiches
- Cheese and onion dip
- Prawn coleslaw dip
- Plain coleslaw
- Crudités
- Rice salad
- Tomato and onion salad
- Lettuce and cucumber salad
- Chicken drumsticks
- Turkey nuggets
- Potato salad
- Mushroom vol-au-vents
- Ritz crackers
- Selected cheeses
- Crisps in several flavours
- Twiglets
- Mayonnaise
- Fruit salad
- Profiteroles
- Fruit mousses
- Chocolate mousse
- Strawberries

Unusual dishes

- Salmon quiche
- Cheese and herb straws
- Tomato and aspic salad
- Salad niçoise
- Potato salad
- Mushroom salad
- Curried prawn vol-au-vents
- Salmon mousse
- Vegetables for dips
- Cream cheese and walnut sandwiches
- Egg and anchovy sandwiches
- Smoked salmon sandwiches
- Asparagus rolled in brown bread
- Avocado and prawn salad
- Prunes rolled in bacon
- Salmon steaks
- Duck pâté
- Liver and bacon pâté
- Mayonnaise with fresh herbs
- Lemon cheesecake
- Strawberry and almond tarts
- Fresh pineapple slices
- Peaches in kirsch
- Ginger mousse
- Coffee gâteau

Appendix F: Wedding anniversaries

Although the word 'anniversary' means a yearly recognition or celebration of an event, many couples in their first year of marriage celebrate every week or month of marriage. Special celebrations, however, are reserved for the annual anniversary on the actual date of the wedding.

Celebrating

The anniversary is, to some, a time to reflect on the past year of marriage, to examine their relationship and take stock. They may celebrate quietly at home – with a candlelit dinner, perhaps – or throw a party for family and friends. The latter is especially true of the 'big' anniversaries: silver (25th), gold (50th) and diamond (60th). Some couples give each other gifts to mark the occasion; other are content merely to mark the day with a special word or gesture.

Traditional gifts

Certain items or materials are traditionally associated with certain anniversary years; often the gifts are made of these materials, or they are in some way related. These vary somewhat, but in general they follow the list below; as the years go by, and the anniversaries grow in number, the gifts become more valuable. Note that for some years there is more than one appropriate category. The list also includes examples of gifts made of the specified material(s).

Traditional anniversary gifts and examples

Anniversary	Material	Example
1	cotton	shirt
2	paper	book
3	leather	belt/gloves
4	flowers	bouquet
	silk	tie
5	wood	breadboard
6	sugar	confectionery
	iron	clothes iron
7	wool	scarf
	copper	saucepan
8	bronze	statue
9	pottery	bowl
10	tin	kitchenware
11	steel	knives/cutlery
12	linen	napkins
13	lace	tablecloth
14	ivory	antique jewellery
15	crystal	vase
20	china	teapot
25	silver	candlesticks
30	pearl	jewellery
35	coral	decorative display piece
40	ruby	jewellery
45	sapphire	jewellery
50	gold	jewellery
55	emerald	jewellery
60	diamond	jewellery
75	diamond	jewellery

Index